For Ludwig von Mises

Andreas Marquart | Philipp Bagus

BLIND ROBBERY!

How the Fed, Banks and Government Steal Our Money

FBV

The Deutsche Nationalbibliothek
Lists this publication in the Deutsche Nationalbibliographie; detailed bibliographic information is available online at **http://dnb.d-nb.de**.

For questions and suggestions please e-mail to
info@finanzbuchverlag.de

1st edition 2016

an imprint of the Münchner Verlagsgruppe GmbH
Nymphenburger Straße 86
D-80636 München
Tel.: +4989 651285-0
Fax: +4989 652096

Translated into English by John Bunch
Editing: Sven Thommesen
Proofreading: Hella Neukötter
Jacket design: Kristin Hoffmann, Munich, Germany
Image on the cover: using iStock-images
Composition: Carsten Klein, Munich, Germany
Printing house: Books on Demand GmbH, Norderstedt
Printed in Germany

ISBN Print 978-3-89879-982-9
ISBN E-Book (PDF) 978-3-86248-907-7
ISBN E-Book (EPUB) 978-3-86248-908-4

Further informations are available at
www.finanzbuchverlag.de

We would like to thank our wives, Eva and Petra,
who lovingly supported us in the months
in which this book was written.

Philipp Bagus & Andreas Marquart

Contents

Preface

Why do the topics of money, inflation, and central banking seem so mystifying? Why do otherwise well-informed people, even those who follow economic and financial news, know so little about how money really operates in society? Why don't we learn anything about money and banking in school? And how does this ignorance leave us vulnerable to political elites and their benefactors in the banking class?

Philipp Bagus and Andreas Marquart have the answers to these questions, and many more, in *Blind Robbery!* The book provides a superb introduction to the vital subjects of money and banking, in an accessible and highly readable style. Students, business people, and even seasoned academics will benefit from their treatment of the origins of money, the monopolizing role of states and central banks, the true nature of inflation, and the terrible economic harms caused throughout history by the political control of currency.

Perhaps most importantly, Bagus and Marquart address the unholy relationship between politicians and bankers in society today. It's a complicated subject, one the financial press scarcely considers. The authors, however, use plain language to explain how legislatures and central banks work together to create a rigged game — rigged against savers, investors, retirees, and anyone hoping to build wealth outside the financial casinos. They illustrate not only the disastrous financial consequences of modern banking systems, but also the moral, cultural, and social impact of punishing thrift and rewarding consumption.

In doing so, the authors carry forward the important work of Adam Fergusson (*When Money Dies*) and Jörg Guido Hülsmann (*The Ethics of Money Production*): societies marked by unchecked monetary expansion inevitably decline in character just as they decline economically.

Throughout the book, the principle and theory behind each argument are presented with admirable clarity. But *Blind Robbery!* is not a theoretical or academic treatise. On the contrary, it's a real-world exposition of modern monetary systems — written with an eye toward helping readers protect themselves from the economic and monetary dislocations our politicians seem hell-bent on creating. Readers especially will benefit from the explication of possible endgame scenarios for fiat currencies in Chapter 8.

Blind Robbery! is a fascinating and enjoyable book — albeit a troubling one — for anyone interested in money and banking in the modern era. Even readers already well-versed in the monetary theory of the Austrian school of economics, will enjoy the authors' fresh approach to the subject. It's a must read for anyone seeking to understand how states and their central banks undermine real prosperity.

Jeff Deist, President, Mises Institute, Auburn (Alabama, USA) March 2016

Introduction: Why this book is so explosive

"The biggest disaster in human history."

That is how economist Roland Baader (1940–2012) describes the state's control over the money supply. This is a bold statement — because almost no one dares to question the state's monopoly on money creation these days.[1]

How about you? Have you ever questioned the monetary system we have? No? Do you think that monopolies are bad? Economists usually describe them as leading to waste, inefficiency, and higher prices. So why should it be any different when it comes to money? Is not money that keeps its purchasing power over time something of great value to everyone? Would you let a state monopoly decide what and how much you eat every day? Of course not. But that is exactly what is happening with money!

If our money is so secure in the hands of the state, then why does it keep losing its purchasing power? You may object that a monetary system controlled by the state is still better than leaving such an important function to the so-called free market. But are you sure? Why is the central bank (the Federal Reserve in the U.S., or the European Central

Bank in the eurozone) allowed to create more and more new money? Why does the state allow the commercial bank around the corner from you to create money out of thin air in the form of credit (loans)? Why is your bank allowed to loan out to others money that *you* have deposited into *your* checking account? After all, you might need that money again soon! When the money is loaned out (and a large portion of it is loaned out), how can it still be available to you when you want it?

What will happen to you if *you* print money? One thing is certain: you won't get past "Go." You won't collect $200. But you will go directly to jail! You see, monopolists don't like competition. They want their monopoly protected.

Based on information from the European Central Bank (ECB), in the eurozone the M2 money supply, which consists of cash, checking deposits, and short-term savings deposits, has doubled since the year the euro was introduced. But if you live in Europe, did the money in your bank account double during that period? No? Did you at least see your income double, then? Again, probably not. Now ask yourself this question: If the money supply in the eurozone doubled, but your bank balances didn't, then is it not reasonable to conclude that the additional money must have ended up in the accounts of someone else? If that person already had more money than you, then he now has *even more.* In this case, the person who started out richer than you has become even richer, and relative to him you have become poorer. In the U.S., the M2 money supply has increased at an even faster pace. From 1999 to 2015, M2 almost **tripled**. Has your American bank account grown three times as large?

But if you expect this book to be a hate-filled rant against the "evil rich" and the CEOs who exploit their poor workers, and who must be forced by law to pay decent wages, or at least a minimum wage, then you would be wrong. Every person — and this includes you — acts from the same motivation. The motivating factor for human action is always the desire to improve one's own well-being and one's own situation.[2]

No one should blame another for seeking to improve his situation by acquiring *more money or more wealth*. It is just human nature. If this motivation were not part of our nature, we would probably still be living in caves. What is important is which means or tools you use to enrich yourself. Some people are more focused than others in their pursuit of wealth, even to the point of using immoral or even criminal means.[3]

If you are of the opinion that people are becoming more and more self-centered and ever less willing to help others, then perhaps the real causes are to be found in our monetary system itself. That is to say, in a monetary system that makes possible the creation of a gigantic, debt-financed welfare state. The welfare state destroys the willingness of people to help each other. Instead of helping someone directly and personally, we push the responsibility onto the state, and tell ourselves, "Well, I already paid enough in taxes."

Do you have the feeling that our society is falling apart? The underlying causes of this are to be found in the nature of our monetary system: this explains why *the few* profit from *the many*, why traditional societal bonds continually wear thin, why people become more materialistic and less caring, why the rich get richer and the poor get poorer. This is why we wrote this book: to explain to you why this is so.

And fear not! You do not need to be an economist to be able to understand this. It is probably even an advantage if you have *not* taken economics classes, since they tend to corrupt your ability to think clearly about economic issues. In any case, what awaits you in this book you would not get in an economics class at a standard government school or university. You just need common sense. We promise.

But let us warn you right now: by the time you have finished this book, you will look upon the world with fresh eyes. So if you think all is right with society and you are happy and content with your life, you can just put this book down right now. Do you really want to read on? Take some time to decide …

Ok. *If you are reading this sentence, you have made the decision to join those courageous enough to learn something new.* Congratulations! You made the smart choice! Only when enough people know about the perversion and the injustice of our monetary system will there be hope for change. *You* are our hope. We are counting on you!

After reading this book, you will see many things from a different viewpoint. That is because you will know what constitutes *good* money, and you will know that our current money is *bad* money. You will see how important good money is for our economy, and what fateful influence *bad* money has on income and wealth distribution in a society. You will understand why the state has seized control of the monetary system and why it wants to hold on to that control.

You will learn why *bad* money always leads to economic downturns and recessions, why banks get into trouble, and why the prices of goods and services always rise.

We will arm you with the knowledge to make you able to tell the difference between *good* and *bad* economic theories and teachings. We also offer our book as an antidote to the very popular tome *Capital in the Twenty-First Century.* This book, written by the French economist Thomas Piketty, generated worldwide buzz and acclaim. According to Piketty's theory, it is capitalism that is responsible for the increasing inequality in income and wealth. What nonsense!

U.S. President Barack Obama, International Monetary Fund (IMF) boss Christine Lagarde, and even the Pope are said to have read Piketty's book. If you happen to see one of them, perhaps you could hand them a copy of **this** book. Otherwise you will be burdened with still more taxes and regulations, which is exactly what Piketty proposes.

You will also learn about the state, government, and politics here. If you have faith in the competence of the state, then it is highly likely that you will lose that faith. And if you have never trusted politicians, you will see your belief confirmed and vindicated here.

And when you have finished reading you will be able to understand why *bad* money is at the core of what is wrong with our society, even extending down to the most basic societal unit — the family. This connection is not immediately recognized because of a tangled web of state interventions, but it exists just the same.

State interventions cover up the true causes of harmful developments in the economy and society, like the application of many layers of paint. Reading this book will allow you to strip away all the layers of paint, and in the end you will be able to recognize, see, and understand the unvarnished truth.

We hope that you enjoy this book.

Philipp Bagus, Andreas Marquart
July 2015

1. Why money does not need the state

"The people will miss those resources in the future that they ate up over the decades."

- Roland Baader

Right from the outset, we would like to clear up a widely held misconception: money was not invented by any one person in particular, and it certainly did not appear as the result of some government decree. Most people know that money is very important, and they believe that it is right and good that the government controls it. Wrong!

Forget for a moment our current monetary system, which we described in the introduction as bad money. Instead, let's begin at the beginning. First, using a simple story, we would like to explain to you how money originally arose. The origin of money illustrates its true nature and shows us what good money is. And when you understand the nature of money, you are ahead of most economists, not to mention most of our politicians.

Imagine a society *without* money. How would trade among people take place? Let's take a trip back in time to a small imaginary city. How far back, we'll leave to your imagination.

Imagine that you live in a small city and you are a shoemaker. You make the best shoes in the area. Unfortunately you don't have any other talents.

Neither you nor your wife can bake bread well. You also don't have any room to keep farm animals. Your children and your wife are widely admired for the shoes they wear. But you can't eat shoes, and thus, from time to time, your wife has to go out and procure foodstuffs. But because money does not yet exist and you only have shoes to offer in trade, your wife is forced to find a farmer who — by chance — needs shoes and is willing to exchange a bag of potatoes or a ham for a pair of shoes. This may work once or twice, but at some point, the farmer does not need any more shoes; his shoe closet is full. When your wife comes by again to exchange shoes for food, the farmer will politely decline her offer.

Let us stop for a moment. Did you notice that we used the word "exchange"? People need a "means of exchange." Our simple example would get more complicated if we included additional professions: a butcher, a blacksmith, a bricklayer. (But notice: no banker! He is not needed here.) How much more could all these people — we will call them market participants — benefit from one another, if they had a means of exchange so that they would not always have to be on the lookout for someone who right then is in need of what they have to offer (whether a pair of shoes, or some dental work, or a plough)? Did you perhaps think to yourself how great it is that we don't have these practical problems, since we have money that is supplied to us by a generous state? If so, we would like to free you from this misapprehension and continue with the rest of our story.

The people in our small city like to adorn themselves with jewelry, particularly gold and silver. It is a long tradition that the men give their wives gifts of gold at every opportunity, when a child is born, when there is a birthday, and at anniversaries.

The women in the city love these presents, but they also know how long their men have to work and how much of their goods or services they have to hand over to the goldsmith to obtain a ring, an earring, or a necklace. But gold is not just a status symbol. Its aesthetic qualities are also indisputable. Gold shines so nicely. Don't you agree? For that reason, in our society, everyone views gold jewelry as something valuable. It is *valued.*

In the meantime, in order to find someone who will exchange potatoes for shoes your wife has again walked so much that she has blisters on her feet — despite her good shoes. She has noticed that small pieces of gold are greatly desired. Pieces of gold are often traded, and people are willing to exchange them for any number of other goods. Or expressed a different way: *Gold is a very marketable good.* It can be exchanged at a favorable rate almost any time. So why not trade the shoes for pieces of gold? One day, your wife gets a bright new idea. Instead of trying to exchange shoes directly for potatoes, she could first trade the shoes for gold and then seek out a potato seller willing to accept her newly acquired gold. Thus, your wife needs, instead of one exchange (shoes for potatoes), two exchange transactions (shoes for gold, then gold for potatoes), but in doing so she could gain valuable time and thereby obtain the desired potatoes with less trouble and effort. Now, perhaps the attempt fails and she is unable to find anyone who will exchange gold for shoes or potatoes for gold. But your wife risks it.

Let us assume that your wife is successful. She obtains the potatoes faster and cheaper by means of an indirect exchange using gold as the intermediate good (medium of exchange). The innovation was successful! From now on, your wife will use this system of exchange for all her undertakings. She will demand gold pieces to be used in exchange. But it is not just your wife who will change her behavior; others will imitate her. Due to the increased demand from market participants, the marketability of gold increases.

This happens because, at her next get-together over coffee, your wife will explain to her friends about her successful "gold-for-potatoes" exchange. As chance has it, a farmer's wife is in attendance. She also has a story to tell. Her husband used the gold that he received from your wife together with some gold from her jewelry case to acquire a new plow from the local smith. The transaction was much easier than usual, since the smith was happy to take the gold. Normally, the smith has such an overabundance of potatoes and hams from exchanges with farmers that he cannot consume all of it before it goes bad, and thus he had no interest in making more plows for farmers.

Word of the new way to exchange goods and services spreads around our small city. More and more, people use gold as an intermediate good rather than exchange goods they have directly for goods they want. Through this, the demand for gold rises and gold becomes more marketable. In other words, it gets more liquid. It becomes a better means of exchange the more market participants demand it and use it — this is a self-reinforcing process. People notice that everyone benefits. They can cooperate more easily, and the division of labor is promoted. Everyone is suddenly relieved of the need to do all the work themselves: each person can concentrate on his or her specific talents instead of spending precious time searching for specific items to exchange.

Everyone can more easily benefit from the abilities of others. Previously, this only took place when someone else required exactly the good or service that another person was ready to offer at the time. With the use of indirect trade, the division of labor can now expand considerably, to the well-being of all.

The monetary system is thus important because the manipulation of it can have a dramatic effect on people's lives and wealth, and because — as Germany's hyperinflation in the Weimar Republic in the 1920s demonstrated — if the monetary system collapses, it is a certainty that the rest of society will also be shaken to its core. Without the use of money, our highly complex economy with its sophisticated division of labor could not be maintained. The division of labor allows for enormous productivity, which in turn allows us to feed a world population of some seven billion people. Without the use of money, most of the current trade in goods and services could not take place, the division of labor would collapse, and people would be forced to attempt to produce everything they needed themselves. The loss of productivity and well-being would be unimaginable. Without a functioning money, the majority of the current population would likely die of hunger and disease. The emergence of money, i.e., a generally acceptable means of exchange, allowed us to establish a complex division of labor and helped the rise of wealthy societies. Stated another way: without money, there can be no civilization.

We should celebrate as heroes those who contributed to the adoption of some goods as money. *Yes, exactly. Your imaginary wife is a hero.* Can we agree that in our small mythical city, *money* has arisen? And did you notice that *no* state was involved, that no government enacted a law that made gold money? Money arose spontaneously in the market place because the market participants who wanted to engage in commerce noticed how useful this was for them. They did not even consciously intend to create money.

Rather, with a monetary good as their means of exchange, they were able to achieve their personal goals better. And because everyone used the same means of exchange — gold — this good became *more* useful.

Money thus has a main function as a medium of exchange. But it also has other functions, such it is also a store of value and can be used as a unit of account.[4] Money can only fulfill its function of holding purchasing power and transporting it into the future if its value is stable. This is because, between the time when your wife sells the shoes for gold, and the time at which you use the gold for purchases, months may go by. Your wife decided in favor of accepting gold pieces in trade because she assumed that they would retain their value during the time in-between transactions. Marketability and value retention go hand in hand. Gold was often used in trade because it was a good store of value. And its frequent use in trade made its value more stable.

A monetary order that arises naturally, that is, without intervention by a state or government, is referred to as a *market monetary system.* It arises without any state coercion. The market participants agree *voluntarily* on the use of certain goods as money, or on multiple goods used side by side. In history, many different goods have been used for this purpose, but eventually market participants tended to settle on gold, silver, or copper. You may have seen old coins in museums, created long before the birth of Christ. If paper money had been in use at the time, the passage of time would have caused most of it to crumple to dust by now. And if there were any paper notes still around, they would only have historical value for collectors. Old coins at least have the value of the metal in them!

What is the reason people throughout history have repeatedly chosen precious metals as money? (Provided no one forced them to use state-issued money.)

Going back in time, when we look at commodity money we find that in the beginning goods used for this purpose were simply regular trade goods (commodities). And because these goods *were frequently traded,* just as in our story, they suddenly became *money or commodity money,* entirely without the involvement of any government or state authority.

But what characterizes this money (which we will call *good money*)? While market participants may have started out using grain or fish for this purpose, why did they tend over time to gravitate towards the use of gold or silver? Very simply: precious metals are rare, divisible, homogenous, cheap to transport and store, non-perishable, relatively easy to recognize and very long lasting. They are constantly in high demand and — above all — cannot easily be duplicated or falsified. (The famous bite into the gold coin we all know from western films.)

In an economy in which there is good money — we will assume it is gold — the quantity of money will only increase when new gold is found. And getting gold out of the ground can only be done with great time and effort. The greatest advantage of gold is that the amount people have dug up since the beginning of time is enormous in relation to the annual production of new gold. In contrast to other goods such as wheat, the yearly gold production is not consumed, rather it accumulates continually. In the past 150 years, the worldwide quantity of mined gold has grown by about 2% per year on average. That is not a lot, and this growth rate has been fairly constant.

What is **not** constant is the rate at which the available quantity of money in our *current* money system is growing. After the introduction of the euro, there were years in which, according to the European Central Bank, the M3 money supply grew by 12%! In the U.S., M3 growth was even higher, reaching 17% in 2008. The M3 money supply is the broadest one; it includes — in addition to cash and demand deposits — longer term time deposits and money market funds. That such high rates of growth are not good for the purchasing power of money, i.e., of *your* money, you can imagine. We will return to this topic in a later chapter.

As you may already suspect, if there is such a thing as *good* money, then there is also *bad* money.

Let us listen to someone who ought to know a lot about money, because he is the president of the German Bundesbank (the German central bank), Dr. Jens Weidmann. In a speech he gave in September 2012, which drew a lot of attention, he said:

> *"The money that we carry in the form of bank notes and coins [he meant the euro — comment by the authors] has nothing to do anymore with commodity money. There has been no direct connection to gold since the U.S. dollar lost its link to gold in 1971. In short: Modern money is not backed by any physical asset anymore. Bank notes are printed paper — those knowledgeable among you know that in the case of the euro, it is cotton, while coins are formed metal. That bank notes and coins are accepted as a means of payment in daily life is partly due to the fact that they are the sole* ***legal*** *means of payment. In the end, the acceptance of paper money primarily is based on the population trusting that they will be able to make purchases later with the paper money that they have."*

You read it yourself: "… has nothing to do anymore with commodity money … not backed by any physical asset anymore … based on the trust of the population."

Interesting, isn't it? The president of the German central bank admits that there are no physical assets behind our money and that the value of our money is solely based on trust.

Many Germans remember the fall of 2008, when the *Hypo Real Estate Bank* was threatened with bankruptcy. People began to lose trust in the monetary system and were withdrawing money from their bank accounts. German Chancellor Angela Merkel and her finance minister at the time, Peer Steinbrück, felt obliged to make a promise to the German people that their savings were safe. Merkel said at the time, "We say to savers, your deposits are safe."

What kind of money is this that politicians have to make such promises guaranteeing its value? The answer is simple: *bad money.* And you can answer the following question yourself without hesitation: do you believe that good money or commodity money is dependent on the guarantees of politicians? We say no.

The money that we use today is bad money and is not based on a voluntary agreement among people. Our monetary system is a pure paper money system. In fact, all currencies worldwide are now pure paper currencies. The last link money had to gold was cut in 1971 when the American president, Richard Nixon, suspended the convertibility of dollars into gold for foreign central banks. (At the time, the exchange value of the dollar was 35 U.S. dollars to an ounce of gold.) Due to increasing indebtedness by the U.S. government, caused to a large extent by the war in Vietnam, mistrust in the dollar grew, and as a result more and more gold was being withdrawn from the vaults of the U.S. central bank. To prevent this, the U.S. government felt it had no alternative other than to suspend the convertibility of the dollar.

As another option to try to regain lost trust in the currency, the government could have tried to reduce spending. But states and governments really dislike fiscal discipline. They greatly prefer distributing money that is not theirs (collected through taxes) to having to tell recipients of government funds that those benefits will have to be reduced!

But back to our topic: today, the state has monetary sovereignty, a monopoly on the creation of money. And monopolies are bad for the consumer, but not for the monopolist. For any other product, consumers would complain about the monopoly position of the producer. But no one does when it comes to money! Why is that? Have *you* ever asked yourself why the government is responsible for our money? Probably not.

When people are asked how much trust they have in their politicians, the results are regularly shocking — at least for German politicians. If the Emnid survey from August 2013 is true, about two-thirds of

Germans have no faith at all in their politicians. How interesting then that when it comes to managing money, we give the responsibility to exactly this professional group! The common man is a bit schizophrenic: we don't trust the politicians, but we expect them to provide us with good money. And when a crisis arises and we begin to lose trust in the money, we still trust what politicians say, namely that our savings are safe. This does not make much sense …

Today, we are capable of incredible technological achievements. We send robot probes to land on Mars and we have smartphones that allow us to send a photo halfway around the world in an instant. Our doctors regularly transplant donated organs. We order things on the Internet in seconds, and — due to masterful logistical achievements — they land on our doorsteps the next day.

However, when the discussion turns to monetary arrangements, we seem to regularly turn off our reasoning abilities. We don't even question our current monetary system, and leave the management of it to politicians we don't trust. We thus hand over the care of our money to people who are apparently unable to even build an airport on time (as shown in the construction of a new airport in Berlin, which has been the subject of embarrassing and costly delays), or keep our highway bridges from falling down, or replace the ancient computer systems operated by the IRS and the FAA in a timely manner. But when the subject is money, the same politicians supposedly really know their stuff! Admittedly, the functioning of our modern monetary system is anything but simple. In addition, it is hidden behind a smokescreen intentionally created so that the normal citizen does not recognize exactly how it works, and thus does not question it. But that is what this book is for — to help you see through the fog.

No one said it better than Ludwig von Mises's student and Nobel Prize winner Friedrich August von Hayek (1899–1992), who wrote in the

1970s that the history of the government's dealings with money is a history of "incessant fraud and deception."

We have seen that for a monetary system to work it is not necessary for the state to be involved. And the notion that it is necessary and important to have a *legally prescribed* means of payment is also not true. History has clearly shown that people can voluntarily agree on what goods they will use as money. They simply need to be left alone for that to happen.

Perhaps you will argue that times are different today, and that a modern economy needs additional money and credit in order to grow. We hear this argument a lot from economists as well as from those who work for the central bank. This claim is also false! An economy will adapt to any quantity of money. More money does not make an economy richer — it just results in higher prices.

Economist Murray N. Rothbard (1926–1995), also a student of Mises's, wrote in his book *What Has Government Done to Our Money?*:

> *"What would happen if, overnight, some good fairy slipped into pockets, purses, and bank vaults, and doubled our supply of money ... Would we be twice as rich? Obviously not. What makes us rich is* ***an abundance of goods****, and what limits that abundance is* ***a scarcity of resources:*** *namely land, labor, and capital. Multiplying coin will not whisk these resources into being. We may feel twice as rich for the moment, but clearly all we are doing is diluting the money supply ... Whereas new consumer or capital goods add to standards of living, new money only raises prices."*

Another error that needs to be done away with is this one: that the more stable the money, the better, and therefore it is a necessary task for the central bank to stabilize the price level. False! Why, you may ask, does the Fed view it as its task to keep prices stable? A counter-question: why does the central bank prevent prices from falling? Just to be clear, we have nothing against falling prices. How about you? But the central bank seems to. Why? Because in a paper money system, falling prices have destructive effects. You will see the reasons as this book progresses.

The purchasing power of commodity money would certainly be more stable than that of our current paper money, and the trend would no doubt be toward more stability. But the purchasing power of commodity money would not be absolutely stable. It would also have swings in value, because it would be closely tied to the fluctuating demand for the monetary commodity (e.g., gold). Sometimes the demand for gold is higher and sometimes lower. Think about it: In times of economic uncertainty, people will want to keep more money, the demand for money will rise, and goods prices will fall — up to the point at which goods prices are again viewed as attractive, uncertainty again declines, and the readiness to exchange money for goods increases.

In times when there is little uncertainty, people will hold less money, the demand for money will be lower, and the prices of goods will tend to rise — up to the point at which they are viewed as too high, and the willingness to exchange money for goods falls again. The central bank, with its self-appointed goal of keeping prices stable, does not allow these natural fluctuations to happen. What it attempts to achieve is to generate *the appearance of price stability*, and to hide the permanent loss of purchasing power of our paper money.

As an aside: the future is always uncertain, just sometimes more and sometimes less. For that reason alone it is necessary to hold at least some money.

We hope that in this first chapter, we have succeeded in motivating you to question received opinion and the status quo!

Summary:

In the absence of state coercion, people agree voluntarily on what good(s) they will use as a means of exchange. In this competitive process, the result is some form of commodity money (good money) as the accepted means of exchange. By contrast, state provided money, which people are forced to use, and whose quantity can be changed at the drop of a bureaucrat's hat, is bad money. Here, we would like to cite again the words of Friedrich von Hayek: "The history of government management of money has, except for a few short happy periods, been one of incessant fraud and deception."

2. Who is allowed to create money and who is not

"Politicians love 'easy money,' because with it, the state and its power elite can go into debt as they wish, without ever having to think of repayment."

- Roland Baader

Having explained what money is, we can now deal with the question of how money is produced. You may also be interested in who is allowed to create money today and who is not. And how the answers to these questions are hidden in the system. In the introduction, we noted the fact that since 1999 the M2 money supply has almost doubled in the eurozone, and almost tripled in the United States.

How does the money supply increase? First we want to look at the production of natural money. "Natural money" is to be understood here as the money supply in a pure commodity money system — for example, where gold and/or silver is used, and in which the supply of money only grows when the supply of new precious metals does. After all, in a free market anyone can mine for gold and silver!

Searching for and finding gold and silver deposits in the ground has always been very time- and labor-intensive, and so is getting it out of the ground. Therefore the growth rate of the available quantity of precious metals has historically been very low. It was exactly this relative scarcity that made gold and silver such excellent means of exchange.

In the past, the production and processing of precious metals was always done by gold prospectors and goldsmiths. Taking into consideration that money is a physical good, and specifically the good with the highest degree of marketability, gold prospectors and goldsmiths did nothing more than produce a market good. No objection can be made to this form of money production, just as none can be made to any other form of goods production that does not violate property rights. And if, in a precious metals-based monetary system, someone was able to produce gold artificially or synthetically, and the result was a considerable expansion of the gold supply and thus of the money supply, then with all probability market participants would abandon the use of gold and move on to using a *different* good as money.[5] In a free market, in which people voluntarily agree — without any state coercion — on *their* money, this would be a completely normal and beneficial process.

Let us return to our imaginary small city from the previous chapter. Remember, gold is the commonly used medium of exchange in our city. An observant goldsmith noticed how people used gold pieces in trade and had the novel idea of smelting down gold and turning it into coins with standardized weights of 1 gram, 5 grams, 10 grams, and 100 grams of gold, with the goldsmith-mint guaranteeing these weights. The mint earned a minting fee for this work, since the coins of standardized weights are more useful in trade than odd-sized lumps of gold.

The people in our city have now become accustomed to handling their commercial transactions with gold. They love being able to exchange their goods *indirectly* using gold coins, rather than *directly*. Commercial exchange has increased considerably, and people have become wealthier.

To begin with, people keep their gold in their homes. As a consequence, some people have misplaced or even lost some of their gold, and there have been burglaries. This becomes a problem. Then one of the market participants, let us call her Anne, has a brilliant business idea, namely to offer a gold storage service. She offers people a place to store their money safely! She has a big safe or a vault installed on her property, and she gives anyone who stores their gold there a warehouse receipt that states the exact amount of gold that was stored. By storing everyone's gold in a big common safe, she can offer secure gold storage at a low price. She charges a fee for this storage service, of course.

People are willing to pay this fee since they no longer have to store their gold insecurely at home. The risk of losing the gold or being the victim of a burglary falls. The warehouse receipts are easier to hide from thieves. Of course, anyone can go to Anne and get their gold back by presenting the warehouse receipt. A simple and ingenious idea!

For this to work, an absolute requirement is that Anne has to have the trust of the other market participants. Her reputation must be above reproach. No one would entrust their gold to a crook! Would you deposit your money with a bank you did not trust?[6]

Anne's business model works. Many people bring their gold to her for storage and obtain their warehouse receipts in return.

Whenever someone wants to make a purchase, they first have to go to Anne to retrieve part of their gold. Then after the sales transaction, the seller takes the newly acquired gold back to Anne for safe storage, and he receives his own warehouse receipt for it. After this has been going on for some time, for the sake of convenience sellers begin to accept warehouse receipts as payment, and then they exchange them for gold as needed at Anne's business. Because Anne has always delivered gold in exchange for warehouse receipts, some people begin to skip the redemption step and just hang on to the warehouse receipts. The paper warehouse receipts begin to circulate, and people start using them as the means of payment (i.e., as money) instead of gold. This is because all of the market participants trust that they can go to Anne at any time with a warehouse receipt and receive gold in return.

After a while fewer and fewer of the market participants come in to exchange their warehouse notes for gold. By far the largest portion of the gold stays in the vault! Anne now begins to think about ways to use this fact to her advantage. She considers getting into the money-lending business. Let us assume that toy merchant Steve deposits 100 grams of gold at Anne's business. Anne now succumbs to temptation and loans out 90 grams of the gold belonging to Steve in cash to homebuilder Hector. BOOM! Did you notice what happened? An almost transcendental act! At this moment, *new money* has been created from nothing. Before Steve deposited his money, he had in his possession 100 grams of gold. Now Steve has a warehouse receipt for 100 grams of gold. He believes that he owns and can spend 100 grams of gold. Because in his eyes, and in the eyes of the market participants, the warehouse receipt is as good as gold — the gold is secure in Anne's vault and can always be redeemed. He can also use the warehouse receipt for purchases.

At the same time, Hector believes he has 90 grams of gold to spend. Both taken together believe, justifiably so, that they can spend 190 grams of gold, and they act accordingly. The money supply (the total quantity of money apparently available in the marketplace) has somehow increased by 90%! This money creation becomes even more evident when we imagine that Anne does not pay out the loan to Hector in physical gold from the vault, but simply issues an additional warehouse note for 90 grams of gold, for which there is no corresponding gold in the vault. The effect is the same.

Anne's new business model becomes an instant success. The market participants gladly accept her loan offers. Previously, in order for a person to get a loan for consumption or investment purposes, someone else had to be ready to forgo the use of his gold or his warehouse receipt. But now, that is no longer necessary. The warehouse receipts are created as if out of thin air. Anne needs nothing other than paper and some ink to make them. What a wonderful business model! Anne creates warehouse notes at little cost to herself and provides them as loans, some of which are paid back using physical gold, and along the way she even gets to charge interest on the loans!

She just has to be careful not to issue too many loans. Why? Because if she did, market participants might become suspicious after noticing that more and more warehouse notes are in circulation. And you know what may happen then. People might lose trust in Anne and then — exactly. A bank run would follow. People would *run* to Anne to exchange their warehouse receipts for physical gold. It should be obvious that the last of them to arrive at the bank would go home empty-handed, because only a fraction of the warehouse receipts would represent gold physically present in Anne's vault (her "gold reserves").

The logical consequence of Anne's business methods is that they serve to *increase the local money supply*. Not only do we have in circulation the warehouse notes that were originally issued when gold was deposited, we now also have the warehouse notes that were created in the process of issuing loans and for which there is no corresponding gold in the vault. We will go into the consequences that come from this later.

One thing is clear: the loans made by Anne represent a **misuse** of the assets deposited with her by her customers. She is making use of the property of others and thus violates their property rights. Her actions are *criminal*, plain and simple.

You should now recognize that the business transactions that Anne is carrying out are very similar to what our banks do today. One could even say that Anne is acting as a bank. Accepting deposits and issuing loans are the essential characteristics of a bank.

You may also have noticed that so far in the story there is no government or state authority in the picture.

The next questions must then be *why* and — most importantly — *how* states and governments throughout history have come to make money production their own affair? The *why* of it is easy to answer. We mentioned it in the first chapter: politicians do not like austerity. Quite the contrary. Anyone who wants to keep the population happy, to buy votes, or to make good on campaign promises, has to have a lot of money available and spend it. But where to get it? Taxes are not exactly popular. They remind the population that state expenses and gifts to voters also cost money and do not magically fall like manna from heaven. What better way to solve the politician's spending problem than by him becoming a partner in the very production of money?

Explaining *how* doesn't take much longer. For a government which is the ultimate authority in a given territory, it is relatively easy to misuse the process of money production for their own advantage.

Imagine that Anne has overdone it with issuing warehouse receipts. After a boom, there will always be a bust. Several market participants can no longer pay back their loans. People begin to doubt Anne's solvency and they start redeeming their receipts for gold. Anne's safe begins to run out of gold. A trickle becomes a raging river. At some point, Anne runs out of gold and is forced to stop redeeming storage receipts. The customers get upset and sue her. In the process, the residing king in the distant capital city is called on to adjudicate the case. He doesn't find Anne's actions to be so bad after all. He thinks the customers can wait a bit. He trusts that Anne will pay back the gold after a time. The customers are very angry, but Anne stays in business.

The economy slowly recovers and Anne starts receiving new gold deposits. She is considering whether to risk issuing new un-backed warehouse receipts again, when the king asks her if he might not get a loan at a favorable interest rate. After all, defending the realm through war is expensive! And does not Anne have a patriotic duty to help out? Of course, Anne cannot say no, and gives the king a loan by issuing fresh warehouse receipts. And thus the game begins anew. An unholy alliance develops between the ruler(s) and the banking system. The king does not defend the property rights of the bank customers, instead he allows Anne to create money out of thin air. In exchange for this, part of the newly created money is given to the state, in other words, to the king.

To illustrate this, two short historical examples should be mentioned. A famous bank which was not a fractional reserve bank was the Bank of Amsterdam, founded in 1609. For about 170 years, all customer deposits in the bank were backed one hundred percent with precious metals. Theoretically, all the customers of the Bank of Amsterdam could have turned up at the same time and demanded their deposits back. No customer would have had to leave empty handed. A bank run would not have been problematic. The bank had a high degree of trust from its depositors. That continued until the 1780s, when the city of Amsterdam needed money to cover its expenses in the fourth Anglo-Dutch War, and requested that the bank lend the city part of its reserves, i.e., part of the customers' deposits.

The second example is the Bank of England, which was founded in the year 1694 in order to finance public expenses. The BoE followed the same path as the BoA, with similar results. This story is described in economist Jesús Huerta de Soto's book *Money, Bank Credit and Economic Cycles.*

There is a key difference in these examples compared to our modern banking system. Back then, even when only a fraction of deposits was held as reserves, the reserves were still in the form of physical gold. Thus, money creation out of thin air had some natural limits. A money note represented a claim to real money, in other words, to precious metal. If there was a bank run, gold or silver had to be delivered, otherwise the bank would have to close its doors. And gold cannot be printed. The danger of gold or silver reserves flowing out was thus an important brake on the creation of money out of thin air. Banks could not become too bold in their actions, because customers could demand to get their gold or silver back at any time.

Today holders of bank notes cannot demand to be paid in precious metal. Recall the speech by the president of the German Bundesbank, Jens Weidmann: *"Modern money is not backed by any physical asset. Bank notes are printed paper — those knowledgeable among you know that in the case of the euro, it is made of cotton."*

Just as a passing thought: just for fun, send a 5-euro note to the European central bank or a 5-dollar bill to the Fed. Include a friendly letter and ask for it to be redeemed. If you receive an answer at all, it will consist of a nice letter and a *different* 5-euro note or 5-dollar bill.

At any rate, history has run its course and you can now understand Hayek's statement that the history of the state's dealings with money is a long history of lies and fraud.

The origins of the symbiotic relationship between the state and the banking system, to the benefit of both, goes far back in history. So far back that most of the people living today know only a paper money system; they do not question it because they have known nothing else.

Ludwig von Mises in his 1949 book *Human Action* wrote:

> *"It is a fable that governments interfered with banking in order to restrict the issue of fiduciary media [bank notes] and to prevent credit expansion. The idea that guided governments was, on the contrary, the lust for inflation and credit expansion."*

Governments gave banks privileges because they wanted to remove the limits that market money puts on credit expansion, or because they were eager to make available to the treasury an additional source of revenue.

Government, as the "ultimate judge," has enacted laws to legitimize exactly those business transactions that we saw as clearly fraudulent in our story of Anne and her gold warehouse. In return, the banks stand ready to contribute to the financing of the state's expenses, by using money created out of thin air in the form of credit.

Ultimately, the introduction of paper money was an essential factor in the state becoming — step by step — the master of money. While previously it was the role of private goldsmiths to mint gold and silver coins, the state now created a monopoly for itself. Step by step, private money providers were driven from the market by legal means.

In order to enable the creation of ever greater quantities of money, the link between paper notes and gold was loosened to a greater and greater degree. People were weaned from the use of gold as cash. The law was used in a targeted way to promote the use of bank notes, and redemption into gold was made harder. Gradually people became used to paper money. At the end of 1944, the Bretton Woods system was founded. At the time, a U.S. dollar could be exchanged for 1/35 of an ounce of gold by any foreign central bank. Private persons however were not allowed to exchange their paper dollars for gold. This system was called the gold exchange standard, and it lasted only until 1971, as we mentioned in the first chapter. And why couldn't this system be maintained either? Because yet again politicians wanted to spend more money than they had available. Even the weak and indirect link to gold inherent in the Bretton Woods system limited the politicians too much in their orgies of spending. So it had to go.

Since 1971 we have been living under a pure paper money system, in which the money supply can in theory be increased without limit. If there is a bank run, limited gold reserves is not a problem anymore. All the authorities have to do is to print the necessary quantity of new paper money. Wouldn't it be fun if we could all play that game, and print as much money as we needed? Yes of course, but we cannot, because the state and the banks like to keep things to themselves, and we are not invited to their party.

The central bank also likes to be thought of as *the lender of last resort*, the *ultimate provider of credit*, and as *a rescuer*. A rescuer who jumps in to help during an emergency, when the banks are in trouble, such as when too many customers attempt to withdraw their money at the same time. In the case of the U.S. central bank (the Federal Reserve System), which was founded in 1913, this lender of last resort was created at the request of the banks. After all, the bankers are not dumb. They know that without a central bank, in the case of a bank run the jig is up. Thus, it is in their interest that there be a central bank. And it is good to know that a central bank can make unlimited liquidity (i.e., money) available when problems arise. Backstopped in this way, the banks can create additional money as aggressively as they like.

By contrast, in a competitive monetary order in which the state does not have its hands in the game, a central bank would be totally unnecessary.

You now know *how* and *why* governments all over the world have taken on and copied this ingenious business model of creating new money out of thin air. By law, they have created for themselves a monetary monopoly together with the entire banking system, including the advantages of monetary creation and money printing. What do you think of this monopoly? Can **you** print money and buy assets with the money you printed? No? But **the central bank** does that. Are **you** allowed to create money on a computer and credit the accounts of others, and earn interest on it in the process? No, but **the banks** can. Why are **they** allowed to do that, but **we** are not? Do you think this is fair? Can a just society be based on such a system? What is cause for concern here is that this state of affairs seems not to bother anyone. People have shown themselves more concerned by the need to build a bridge for frogs to cross a highway than by the need for a private banking system. At least, they have been up until now, as shown in the 37 bridges built for animals in Germany.

Now, we would like to look at how money arises in the banking system in more detail.

At your leisure, do the following test: ask a friend or acquaintance if he or she knows where the permanently expanding money supply comes from.

The answer that you will receive will — almost certainly — be: "The central bank prints the money" or "the Fed prints the money."

The answer is even partly correct. It is true that the central banks print money. But not only in paper form, as the pictures from the German Weimar hyperinflation in 1923 show, where people pushed wheelbarrows full of money around. Today, central banks create money electronically in the form of bits and bytes. That is cheaper. They don't even need paper and ink, as Anne from our imaginary city did. The central banks inject this electronic money into the banking system to support the creation of credit and to "improve liquidity," as it is expressed in official press releases. Central banks are akin to modern day gold prospectors producing at virtually zero costs.

The creation of new money by central banks is often referred to as "monetary policy," which officially aims at maintaining "price stability." However, the main effects for central bank money creation are two. First, central banks save and support the banking system, which indirectly finances the political class and their favorite policy schemes. Second, central banks create money to finance the government even more directly. This happens when a central bank buys government bonds, i.e., government debt. The central bank may buy the bonds from the government or from the banking system. In both cases the government receives a bank wire transfer directly to its accounts. In exchange for the newly created money, the central bank receives government bonds. The new money for this transaction comes directly from the government's printing press, or more precisely from the central bank's computer.

In the jargon of economists this process is called "the monetization of debt." That may sound terribly noble, but it isn't better because of the name. Governments have their central banks create money, then have the money wired to themselves, and then they buy all kinds of stuff with it: iPads for their employees, plush new offices, a fleet of luxury vehicles, or they rescue some other country's government from bankruptcy using the argument that there was no alternative.

Most people believe that new money is *only* created by the central banks. But that is incorrect. The biggest part of money growth takes place in the banking system itself, including your savings and loan and the credit union around the corner.

There is another test you may try on anyone that you know. Most likely, a conversation like the following will result:

> "What does your local bank do with the money that is in your checking account?"
> "They work with it."

"Yes, but what does the bank do with it, *exactly*?"
"They invest it."
"Ok, but *how* does the bank invest it?"
"I don't know."
"Why do you think that the money is still in your account, when the bank is using it for its own purposes?"
"I don't know that either."
"You have the money in your checking account. Why in checking rather than a savings account?"
"Because I may need it on short notice."
"Is it ok if your bank invests your money, whatever they are doing with it, when you may need it on short notice?"
"Not really, but I don't care, so long as I can get to it at any time."

Given such a lack of understanding, it is high time to clear the air. We live with a fractional reserve banking system. This means that your bank is allowed — by the highest authorities, in other words with legal permission from the government banking authorities — to *loan out your money*. It merely has to maintain a minimum required reserve ratio, and in the U.S. that is — you might want to sit down — about *10%*. Again: 10%. Let's assume that you have $10,000 in your checking account. Your bank may, theoretically, loan out $9,000 of that. Your bank only has to hold $1,000 as a *reserve* in cash, or they may park the equivalent amount in an account at the central bank. Your bank is thus acting exactly as Anne did in our imaginary city, when she loaned out 90 grams of gold out of every 100 grams deposited.

You may now object and say, "I don't care, so long as I can withdraw it at any time." Let's just allow that to stand without comment for now. When you are done reading this book, hopefully you will know more, and care.

Let's assume that your bank lends $7,000 of the $10,000 in your account to your neighbor. She signs a loan contract at the bank, and the next day she takes a look at her bank statement to see if the loan has been credited to her account. You see her by chance in the lobby of the bank. She has her statement in her hand, the loan went through and her account now shows a balance of $7,000. Your own statement shows that you still have $10,000. If the money were no longer there in full, you would immediately protest, right? Let us do some quick arithmetic: $7,000 plus $10,000 makes $17,000. But before your neighbor got her loan from the bank, there was only *your* $10,000 on hand at the bank!?!?

You will no doubt agree that we are now entitled to ask where those extra $7,000 came from, since they did not exist yesterday. The answer is as short as it is incredible: *Out of nowhere!*

You have just witnessed how *new money* is created.

You now know *how* our money is created, and you can understand why our paper money is called *fiat money*. If you know a little Latin you have no doubt already translated that phrase in your head. Almost everyone knows the phrase from The Bible, as God created the Universe: He said, *"Fiat Lux,"* which is translated as: *"Let there be light."* In other words, *Fiat Money = Let-there-be money:* what is money is money by someone's decree, not because it was freely chosen by market participants.

At this point, you may not be able to see what important negative effects this money creation process has on the purchasing power of your income and your wealth, and even on your private life, and because you are not alone, on the entire society. But this book will tell you. We promise.

Do you think that the game is over at this point? Not a chance. Let's go back to your neighbor's bank statement, which showed a balance of $7,000 after she received her loan. Let us assume that she will be making purchases with this money. Taking out a loan just to let the money sit in her account would not have made much sense. She decides to remodel her kitchen, and she transfers the money for that purchase to the seller. The money is deposited to the account of the kitchen renovation firm. At the same bank or at a different bank, that doesn't make any difference here. At any rate, the money creation process continues apace. Let us assume that out of the $7,000 deposited by the kitchen renovator the bank lends $5,000 to a guy who wants to purchase a car. His checking account is credited with $5,000. Let's do the math: you still have $10,000 in your account, the kitchen renovator has $7,000, and the prospective car buyer has $5,000 in his account. If the car purchase is made and if the seller of the car deposits $5,000 at her bank, the game can go on to the next round. Let us assume that the car seller's bank provides a $3,000 consumer loan to a customer who wants to buy a new flat-screen TV. After the sale, the seller of the TV deposits the amount into his checking account. Now, the checking accounts hold a total of $10,000 plus $7,000 plus $5,000 plus $3,000. The original $10,000 deposit has now grown to $25,000! And we could continue on from there. But that won't be necessary. We do not want to waste your time, or ours. You can see that as the process goes on, the total amount of money grows, while the amounts of newly created money become smaller and smaller.

In our example, we have assumed a relatively large reserve ratio. Out of the $10,000 in the initial step, only $7,000 were loaned out. Implicitly, this represents a reserve ratio of 30%. Let us instead use the Fed's required reserve ratio of 10%. From the initial $10,000, not $7,000 but up to $9,000 are lent, then at the next step $8,100, then $7,290, and so on. (Each step is 90% of the previous step.) Mathematically, this is an infinite series which has a convergent sum. In the extreme case, an initial $10,000 could grow to become $100,000. The banking system would then have created $90,000 out of thin air. It maintains a cash reserve of $10,000 (namely, your initial $10,000 deposit), in other words, 10% of total deposits.

By comparison, the required reserve ratio in the eurozone is only one %!

At this point in the explanation, a common objection raised is that through the purchases or investments made with the borrowed money, new goods are produced, or put more simply, "the economy grows." That may be, but we will prove to you in this book that sustainable, real wealth cannot be created from *nothing*. It is also hard to imagine that it could be. It would be too good to be true! Let us take this "We are making money out of thin air and creating wealth with it" model to its logical conclusion: We simply create billions and billions of dollars of new bank notes and distribute them to everyone. Soon everyone would have so much money that they would not need to work anymore! But we both know that in the real world this quite simply cannot work: who would then be producing the food and other goods we need?

Our coercive state monopoly monetary system is the biggest case of fraud in human history. Let us be more precise: it is fraud **against the people**. And if — as mentioned in the introduction — **your** bank account has not tripled in the last 15 years, then **you** are one of those cheated. *You* are cheated by having your income and your purchasing power stolen and your personal property violated.

And this takes place in a hidden manner through an obscure process so complex that almost no one understands it. Henry Ford (1863–1947), the founder of the Ford Motor Company, put it this way: It is well enough that people of the nation do not understand our banking and monetary system, for if they did, I believe there would be a revolution before tomorrow morning.

Summary:

Our money is no longer linked to or backed by any physical commodity. Modern fiat money is created from nothing, out of thin air. It is created partly by the central bank (when it purchases government bonds or other assets) and partly by the banking system itself (through the fractional reserve multiplier process we described above).

The monetary system is regulated by the government, and in fact the state has the legal monopoly on the creation of new money. The state and the banks that help finance it are in a position to benefit greatly from this monopoly.

3. Why our current money creates social injustice

"Few people really understand to what extent — over generations — the combination of the progressive income tax and inflation has robbed them of the fruits of their labor."

- Roland Baader

Rarely have definitions created such confusion as in the case of the terms "inflation" and "deflation." Inflation comes from Latin and means "to blow up" (as in inflating a balloon). And deflation comes from "deflare" and means "to drain" (as in deflating the balloon).

Ask some friends what they understand inflation to mean. *Inflation is when everything becomes more expensive.* This or something similar will almost certainly be their answer. Now, definitions are not true or false in and of themselves. We use them as tools of thought. But a definition can be inappropriate when applied to a given subject, and can even cause confusion.

Until about the middle of the 20th century, *inflation* was understood as **an expansion of the money supply**. The opposite also applied. *Deflation* meant **a decrease in the money supply**, not a period of falling prices. Only with the ascent of economist John Maynard Keynes (1883–1946) did the modern equating of inflation with more expensive goods arise.

Enter "inflation" in Google as a search term and you will be surprised. In most of the search results, the concept is interpreted as increasing prices.

Even in a pamphlet put out by the European Central Bank for a younger audience — under the title *Price stability: why is it important for you?* — it states, *"Inflation is understood as a general or broad rise in prices for goods and services over a longer period of time, which leads to a decline in the value of money and to a loss of purchasing power."*

The definition of deflation is along the same lines — well, at least they are consistent. The following statement can be found in the same brochure: *"Deflation exists when the general price level falls over a longer period of time."*

When so many people and even the experts (and the people from the ECB are surely experts) have forgotten the traditional definition of inflation as an expansion of the money supply, or when they choose to ignore it, then it is fair to ask ourselves whether we are being intentionally misled. One is inclined to assume that they don't want everyone to understand that the money supply is being continually expanded. No one questions why everything becomes more expensive. Because after all, people have become so used to it. Virtually no one asks what the actual reasons for the price increases are. "That's just the way it is. Everything gets more expensive. Do you know what a scoop of ice cream used to cost? 10 cents."

Defining inflation as an increase in the prices of goods and services deflects attention away from the real reasons. It is much easier to blame others. Then it becomes the evil capitalist ice cream vendor or the greedy oil baron who have raised prices to enrich themselves.

Defining inflation as an increase in prices is like confusing a symptom with the underlying illness. But it is not the fever that is the cause of the illness, it is the viruses in the body. In just the same way, the rising prices is merely the result of monetary expansion. It is not even a necessary consequence. It would be easy to come to the wrong conclusion that if there are no price increases, everything must be ok. This would be very wrong. Even if the prices *do not* rise there can still be an increase in the money supply, compensated for by other factors such as a rise in productivity due to innovation, and/or an expansion of the division of labor.

Today's common understanding of inflation diverts attention away from the expansion of the money supply. Even if prices do not rise or rise only slightly, increases in the money supply have their typical results, which we will discuss later in this book.

Why people got away from the original inflation definition, understood as increases in the money supply, may now be clear. Someone might ask, "Well, where does all this money actually come from?" It looks like they don't want us to look too closely. Not everyone needs to know that money is created out of thin air, goes the thinking. At the end, the citizen might want to know why they need to work for their money while others create it with a snap of their fingers.

So just for the record, again: *We define inflation as an expansion of the money supply; the concept of deflation means a reduction of the money supply. Rising prices are a result of inflation, as measured, for example, by the monthly consumer price indexes published by the government (the Bureau of Labor Statistics in the U.S., bls.gov).* More later on the consumer price index.

In Europe, the experts at the European Central Bank have even come up with a goal for the growth of the money supply: 4.5% per year. This is a "reference value," the rate that they would like to see the money supply grow by every year in the eurozone.

But *more money does not make a society richer.* If our central bankers believed that it did, then why don't they stop being so modest and let the money supply grow by 10% per year, or 20%, or why not even 100% per year? Suggest to the Fed that they should call in all the dollar notes, coins, and bank accounts and replace the numbers on them by adding a zero to the end. The money supply would be ten times bigger. Those calling for more money and an expansive Fed policy would be overjoyed. Maybe they would even win the Nobel Prize in economics for their idea. A prize of 8,000,000 Swedish kronor, which is about $940,000 (or even $9,400,000 after our monetary expansion!). Imagine that. It would be worth a try, right?

But seriously. Would society really become richer as a result of such a monetary expansion? Would there be more cars, more real estate, groceries, and arts, movies and theater offerings? No. The only thing that would happen by putting this idea into practice is that the prices would become ten times higher. The opposite also applies. If they took a zero off all bank notes and coins, society would not be poorer. Real goods would not have disappeared. Only the money supply would have contracted to one-tenth its former size. The purchasing power of the remaining dollars would have expanded by a power of ten.

This shows that *any* quantity of money is optimal for purposes of fulfilling the exchange function of money. If a zero is added to the end of the numbers printed on bank notes, the price level will go up by a factor of ten. If a zero is removed, they go down to one-tenth. But the dollar would not be a better or a worse money. This should put to rest the persistent falsehood that the money supply needs to "adapt to the supply of goods" or that the economy needs a "rising money supply to grow." In reality, some economists are still attached to these falsehoods and proclaim them as an argument for a paper currency. They fear that economic growth without (sufficient) monetary growth could bring production to a standstill. Wrong. If more is produced, prices will fall without an expansion of the monetary supply. For companies, that is not a problem; they would produce and sell more too. *Falling prices are the natural result of economic growth.* This is the natural way for most people to take part in advances in productivity. That would only be fair, don't you think? But those in power always try to prevent falling prices. Why?

Price deflation phobia reigns supreme. What is overlooked is the fact that falling prices do not have to be a problem for enterprises. What is decisive for enterprises is their margin, in other words the difference between their input prices and their output prices. If the input prices fall faster than the output prices, the margins will even increase, as is the case today in the technology sector.

It is indeed true that people in debt lose out when prices fall unexpectedly, and can be forced into bankruptcy if they happen to be over-indebted. But from the perspective of the overall economy, that is not so problematic. Redistribution simply occurs. Creditors who have better foreseen the price development take over that bankrupt enterprise and become its new owners. But this change of ownership does not affect the productive capacity of the economy as a whole, because the factories, streets, machines, and workers still exist.

What a clever strategy: To claim that falling prices would be a catastrophe and to propose as the solution … well, you can predict what that will be. Right: an expansion of the money supply. And the new money should come to those proposing this, thank you very much. Then the economy will supposedly also prosper. This phobia against falling prices is meant to legitimize inflation. And with inflation debtors profit at the cost of savers and creditors. Those who obtain the new money first are the winners.

And this brings us to the *effects* of inflation. What does inflation mean for you, for your income, for your wealth? What effects does inflation have on income and wealth distribution within a society? You will now understand why we called this book *Blind Robbery! How the Fed, Banks and Government Steal Our Money.*

Because you are familiar with our imaginary small city by now — you already know some of the city's inhabitants — we will now return to it.

Gold as a commodity money has proven itself as an excellent means of exchange in our imaginary city. We will assume that our storage entrepreneur Anne works in a manner that is above reproach, in other words she no longer issues excess warehouse receipts against the money in her vault. And after massive citizen protests, the king no longer interferes with the monetary system.

The gold prospectors look for gold every day, but new finds are very rare and small. Gold in the ground, which makes prospecting and digging profitable, appears to have dried up. Thus the gold supply only increases at a very low annual rate. The people in the city are hardworking and because the quantity of goods produced is always increasing, while the quantity of gold remains almost the same, the purchasing power of gold continually rises. The prices of goods fall.

Almost everyone is happy, except the gold prospectors. Some of them have gotten together and worked on a new kind of drill which they will use to look for gold in ever deeper rock layers. One day, one of the prospectors comes up with the idea of putting a special steel tip on the drill that will not wear out, even when drilling through hard rock. Initial tests are carried out and it works.

The group of prospectors can now drill much deeper, and the first attempt meets with success. They hit many gold formations at depths that they were not able to reach before. They now know that their mining efforts will be profitable and they are able to find large quantities of gold, quantities that exceed previous production quantities, and that are greater than the quantities achieved by their colleagues working with traditional drills.

Our gold prospectors get a goldsmith to turn the gold they found into coins, and now they have amounts of money that they would not have dreamed of a short time before. They use their money to invest extensively to expand their production even further.

They purchase large areas of land under which they suspect there may be large gold deposits. They purchase additional machines such as rock-grinders and trucks, they build new warehouses, expand their production facilities, and hire new miners. And because our gold prospectors are forward-looking entrepreneurs, they begin to invest in other sectors by buying shares in other companies. As a result, share prices start to rise.

What the gold prospectors do not know at the moment is that with their gold finds they have put themselves into a really comfortable position. In the beginning, they are able to make all of their purchases and investments at yesterday's prices, because the new money flows into the market *for the first time.*

If a prospector finds new gold, he is the first recipient and the winner in the monetary increase game. This is because the gold prospector can make purchases with his new money at the old, still unchanged prices. If he and his friends buy more beer in their favorite bar located right next to the mine, then the beer prices will have a tendency to rise. The next person to benefit is the bar owner who profits from the money supply increase — if somewhat less than our fortunate gold prospector. Due to increased income, the bar owner now has more money. And he can spend the money himself to buy roses for his wife, for example. The price of roses increases. The new money makes its way to the florist, who spends it. The money slowly is distributed throughout the economy. Prices rise.

Just as the prospector, the bar owner, and the florist benefit from the monetary expansion, there are others who lose, because the money only gets to them later. They have to pay higher prices for beer, flowers, and other goods, before their income rises. To make the redistribution specific: the beer that the later recipient of the money used to be able to buy and which he cannot afford to buy now, is instead enjoyed by the gold prospector.

In 1949, Ludwig von Mises described the effects of the changed money quantities in his book *Human Action*:

> *"Every change in the money relation alters — apart from its effects upon deferred payments — the conditions of the individual members of society. Some become richer, some poorer ... If an inflationary movement and a deflationary one occur at the same time or if an inflation is temporally followed by a deflation in such a way that in the end prices are not very much changed, the social consequences of each of the two movements* ***do not cancel each other****. To the social consequences of an inflation are added those of a deflation."*

What lessons can be learned from what happened in our city? *The answer is simple: income and wealth were redistributed.* The gold prospectors became richer. Those who were second or third in line to receive the new money also gained, but less. All those who obtained the new money later became relatively poorer. The true losers from the increase in the quantity of money are those whose income grew slower than the prices. Those who were harmed the most were those who were the last to enjoy the new money, or who obtained none of it.

By the way, what happens when the new gold fields run dry? Or when the new money is not produced in as high a volume as before? Then the economic structures created by the expansion of the money supply will be unable to withstand the test of time. The bar owner now has fewer sales, and so does the person selling roses.

If the bar owner expanded his bar during the boom time, he will now have financial problems, because there will be fewer miners buying his beer.

The new mines now become ruins — the ghost towns of the American West are an example. After the gold was exhausted there, the structures that were built up with a lot of time and effort were written off as malinvestments and abandoned. The same occurs in the modern paper money system, which leads to investments that are not in tune with long-term consumer demand. These projects and investments will also be written off at some point as malinvestments, just like the "ghost towns" on the periphery of big Spanish cities that were built during the recent real estate bubble. If paper money production is slowed down, it will become evident that many enterprises were only created as a response to monetary production, and thus took funds away from other projects. But more on business cycle theory in the next chapter.

Back to inflation. When the money supply is expanded — or inflated — it is of critical importance who gets to use the new money first. The first recipients of the new money have clear advantages over the later recipients and of course over the last recipients. Those who obtain the new money first can make purchases at prices that have not started going up yet. As Murray N. Rothbard explains in his book *What Has Government Done to Our Money?*, the money then expands step by step through the economy and causes the prices of goods to rise.

Those who get the money last are the losers in this game. They can only buy at increased prices and receive less and less for their money.

If you are a wage earner, a salaried employee, or a retiree, then you should probably view yourself as one of the losers. By the time the newly created money gets to *you*, the first recipients have already invested it. They have bought real estate and invested in corporate stock. By the time it is your turn, the real estate that you would have liked to buy is now too expensive. The money that you saved for years is no longer enough. If we wanted to be cynical, we could have said, *real estate has gotten too rich for your money.* But the effects of *bad money* are much too serious to be cynical about. And if you now decide to invest in the stock market instead, the stock market will be at a level where the first recipients have already gotten out — having realized big profits.

But who are these first recipients to whom the new money flows first? Primarily, it is the government, the banks, and large companies and corporations. They are the ones who get their hands on the newly created credit money before you do. But they are also borrowers who are ready to take on debt in order to procure goods or for investment purposes. The *new* money thus flows to them *before* it does to you.

We do not at all want to blame those who are merely taking on debt and who have no responsibility for the way that our monetary system is designed. They are merely acting rationally. They strive to earn profits and to improve their wealth. The task of entrepreneurs and managers is to make products and services available that customers want to buy. And to be able to do that, investments in development, production, and sales are necessary.

Often, they do not have the necessary capital to fund their projects, and that makes taking on debt necessary. Nevertheless, *bad money* also has negative effects for enterprises. We will discuss this in a later chapter.

A small aside: The effect triggered by the increase in the money supply resulting in a redistribution of wealth is called the *Cantillon Effect*, named after the Irish banker Richard Cantillon (1680–1734), who witnessed the results of a massive monetary expansion on a "live subject." It was during the time when the French massively expanded their money supply based on a suggestion by Scottish financier John Law (1671–1729). This expansion led to a financial bubble related to the French Mississippi Company, and it burst — as all paper money bubbles do — and many investors were ruined by it. As a result, the term "bank" was for a long time synonymous with "fraud" in France. The people of France suffered for decades from the devastating effects of Law's paper money experiment.

It was an exciting time in which Cantillon and Law lived. Today is also exciting — and rest assured, it will remain exciting and will get *even more* exciting. It is possible that the term "bank" in the not too distant future will also trigger negative associations like that.

But back to the topic at hand: Because new money does not reach the market participants at the same time (and fails to reach some at all), income and wealth are redistributed massively within a society, and the tendency is for that to be **from** those at the bottom **to** those at the top: **from** wage earners, salaried employees, and fixed-income retirees and **to** the government, the banks, (large) companies, large-scale investors and to those already rich. That is because whoever already has assets can use those as security for additional loans, in order to obtain more real estate and shares of companies while credit is cheap.

For sure, rich people are more easily able to gain access to the new money created out of thin air. The result is clear. According to the fourth German poverty and wealth report of the German government of 2013, the lower 50% of households have only about 1% of total net assets, while the 10% of richest households have 53% of total assets. Expressed another way, the 10% richest households have more net assets than the other 90% combined. And the chasm is growing. Since 1998, the share of the 10% richest households — relative to total assets in the economy — has grown by 8%.

Inflation results in an unjust distribution of wealth in an economy. You certainly will have noticed that we have avoided the fuzzy term "social justice" here. While everyone has a clear idea of what just actions are, specifically to not kill, cheat, or steal, the term "social justice" is vague. It can mean almost anything. And the term is often used to justify something that is deeply unjust, for example the expropriation of legally gained property by means of taxes. So whenever you hear the term "social justice," make a quick check to be sure that your wallet is still there.

By installing and establishing a state monetary monopoly, it is ultimately the state that forces a redistribution that favors the super-rich. But those also profit who receive the new money from the state as second- and third-level recipients, before the prices really start to climb. For example, bankers who are bailed out, and their managers, foundations that receive money, as well as subsidized solar power companies — indirectly, a whole army of state dependents. It is mainly the productive, hard-working citizens who save who come out empty-handed.

The average uninformed citizen who is forever manipulated by left-wing propaganda is of course told that it is evil capitalism that harms society and that capitalism therefore must be reined in. So: the workings of state money and the state-privileged banking system result in the super-rich becoming even richer and the lower class and middle class being forced into relative poverty. And, irony of ironies, the state then reappears, throwing around the term "social justice," forces itself on people as an un-asked-for rescuer, and engages in a further bit of redistribution. That is like making the arsonist responsible for tossing a cup of water on the fire he started. We will discuss how the state exploits the lack of knowledge of the average person later in this book.

Coerced redistribution is not only deeply unjust, it also creates social conflicts. Everywhere there is social conflict today, we find an underlying redistribution battle as the cause. Either the losers of the redistribution want less redistribution, or the winners want more. But the most common case is that the redistribution is reduced and the subsidy "junkies" mobilize and protest in the streets. This happens whether it is the reduction of agricultural subsidies, a reduction in welfare payments, the introduction of tuition at public state universities, or a reduction in pay for bureaucrats in countries such as Greece. It is always about redistribution and it always results in social conflicts.

The same thing does not happen in the free market. Have you ever seen a mass demonstration in a big city because Apple changed its prices, introduced a new product, or when its employees did not receive a pay raise? Anyone who dislikes Apple's strategy can just go to work for the competition. In a free market, all decisions are voluntary. Only when redistribution and coercion come into play does harmony end. The redistribution that takes place through the monetary system also promotes conflicts, particularly when the redistribution is obvious, as seen in the recent eurozone bailouts, in which the Germans were the main losers. In the United States, ordinary people are the losers from the Fed's "quantitative easing."

And the southern Europeans, who have become dependent on subsidies, march in protest against any cuts to their welfare states as they blame the Germans, because the Germans do not want to crank the money faucet of the ECB wide open. In short: redistribution through the euro system provokes conflicts among nations and endangers the peace in Europe.

We now want to consider what effects the enormous gold findings by our gold prospectors have in our small city, when the following scenario occurs.

Some citizens of the city are real geniuses. They have made critical technological advances in many areas. The best advances were in product manufacturing and logistics. Through the pioneering invention of the wheel, transport companies in particular now have many useful applications. The division of labor can be extended more cheaply. A majority of enterprises immediately use the newly developed technology, and the productivity in the city is enormously boosted. The profits of the companies rise, because with less effort, considerably more goods and services can be offered and sold than before.

Now you might think that many workers and employees will no longer be needed and will be unemployed, because when companies boost their productivity through new technologies, they end up needing fewer workers. That is true. But does that mean that no new technologies should be introduced? Please! That would be nonsense. Consider the enormous technological advances that mankind has made throughout history: the wheel, the steam engine, plastics, computers, the nuclear power plant, the self-driving car … If every technological advance had created new, long-term unemployment, then by now we would have legions of unemployed, right? Correct. The invention of the wheel meant no more need for load-haulers. But all the wheels and coaches now needed do not fall from heaven, someone has to build them. Thank God that those former load-haulers *are* still around.

Generally, the desires of people are unlimited. Many of these desires go unfulfilled, because there are not enough workers, or because not enough can be produced. Due to the invention of the wheel and the re-employment of the load-haulers, now many of those unfulfilled wishes can be fulfilled. The productivity of the economy grows thanks to new technology and capital accumulation.

Through the improved productivity and the resulting increase in the production of goods (please note that the money supply remains unchanged), prices in the city begin to fall. People can now afford things that they could not afford before. The people who used to work as load-haulers begin to create a myriad of service firms that do the work that people did themselves prior to this, and which others can now do for them. Or they find new work in newly created sectors where products are manufactured which were not produced before in large quantities, because people quite simply could not afford them. *Now* the people of the city can afford considerably more, because the prices have fallen. Falling prices! What a concept!

But wait. Before the prices start to fall, our gold prospectors come into play. Yes, the people who found a lot of gold. How nice it could have been without those guys! (Transferred to our monetary system of today, "those guys" are the central bank — the Fed or the ECB.)

Just as described, their new money flows into our small city and prevents the attained productivity increases from unleashing their price-lowering effect. The dream of falling prices and being able to afford more than ever is now over.

And the gold prospectors again obtain their advantage from the fact that they had the newly created money *first*. And the unfortunate losers are those who receive the new money last. Only this time, it is less obvious who is who, since the prices do not rise. But redistribution is still happening.

Now back to present reality. It is certain that in the past 30 years, due to technological advances such as those in the IT sector, and due to China and India now taking part in the international division of labor, prices should have fallen by maybe 30 to 40%. But prices have increased. Can you (and better yet, do you dare to) imagine the enormous increase in money supply and the enormous redistribution of wealth that is responsible for this?

The Fed is even so bold as to claim that prices have been kept virtually stable for a long time. So for some years, extremely low rates of price inflation have been reported. (For the ECB, "price stability" is defined as annual price increases of up to 2%! Truly an abuse of language.) But prices would have fallen without the immense money production by the Fed and other central banks. The rate by which the prices unfortunately did *not* fall because of monetary expansion would have to be added to the reported rate of price inflation. The rate of price inflation that would then have to be shown would certainly be considerably higher than what we have today. A loss of confidence in our paper money system would happen so much faster if that were the case. And the fiat money profiteers of course want to prevent that. A parasite can live from the host so much better, in that way. Sounds pretty harsh, right? But it is that way … unfortunately.

You can translate both scenarios from our small city — with a few exceptions — to our current paper money system. The main difference is clear. It has to do with *how* the new money entered our city, specifically through gold finds, and how new money enters the economy today — specifically, it is created out of thin air.

If people in a commodity money system — such as a currency based solely on gold — fear that immense quantities of new gold are likely to be produced, they would very quickly turn to another *commodity*, perhaps silver, or platinum. We don't want to speculate, the market participants would simply, as time went on, spontaneously start using a *different* means of exchange. And they would be doing so in the complete absence of any coercion by the state.

In our current state-run money monopoly, on the other hand, people cannot escape the situation. One flood of money after the next — created by the Fed and the banking system — washes over the people. They witness in desperation as their income and wealth continually lose value.

An additional important difference between a gold-based currency and paper money is in the probability and the extent of inflation. In a pure gold currency large increases in the money supply are rare. Even when the 16th century Spanish Conquistadores brought stolen gold treasure back from the Americas to the Old World, it took an entire century before the quantity of money in Europe had doubled. (This translates into an annual growth rate of about 0.7%.) Since then, the quantity of gold has grown by between 1 and 2% per year. This is very different from the current paper money system. For example, in 2007, the U.S. M2 money supply grew by almost 12%. Growth at that rate means a doubling of the money supply every six years!

An additional difference between gold in our example city and our current paper money is that everyone has the right in our city to acquire land and to prospect for gold on it. But today, not just anyone can acquire a money press and print euros or dollars.

A monopoly exists. And the monopolist does not have costs. While the gold prospectors have to test and experiment with new techniques to invent something like a new drill, and take on very high costs and risks, our current money supply can be multiplied by a factor of ten at the press of a button. The temptation to use the money production privilege is almost irresistible and explains the high rate of monetary growth. Try it on your computer. Open an Excel document and name it "My account." Type in a 1 and a lot of zeros before the dollar symbol. Not hard at all, is it? The Fed can do exactly that, and does so in order to buy up government bonds or to give credit to banks at low interest rates. Or the ECB puts up a new office complex in Frankfurt for over a billion euros in total construction costs.

The effect of *new, additional* money is always the same. Not only when the money supply is expanded and causes price increases, but also when the money supply is expanded during a time in which the prices for goods and services otherwise would fall. In both cases, income and assets in a society are redistributed. And the tendency is for that to happen from the bottom to the top. And it cannot be reversed. It is, so to say, sustained and long term.

Between 2000 and 2012 the M2 money supply in the U.S. increased by about 100%, while real output in that same period only increased by about 24%. *100%.* Can you imagine the extent of the redistribution behind that figure? It is surely massive. The widely held (but erroneous) opinion of economists is that the money supply must be flexible and must grow at a rate that tracks the rate of economic growth. The above growth rate of the money supply, which far exceeded that of real economic output during the same period, thus ought to have triggered storms of protest from the economics profession. Have you seen anyone protesting it so far?

We are convinced that you will now agree with us when we make the following statement: *monetary expansion (inflation) is partly responsible for the increasing schism in society between rich and poor. It is responsible for the fact that more and more people cannot live on the wages they earn and that families can no longer pay for their living expenses from the income of a single wage earner.*

But you will never read a statement like that from a central banker or from a bank manager, and you also won't ever hear it from a politician.

From the point of view of the state and the money producers, it is definitely not desired that people understand what influence the *money created out of thin air* has on their lives. Have you ever witnessed a con man explaining to his victim during the con job the tricks that he is using?

Summary:

Inflation leads to a redistribution of income and wealth in a society. Inflation favors those who are the first to obtain the newly created money. They profit and are able to acquire goods at yet unchanged prices. Those who obtain the new money only later are the victims. At the point when they receive more income, the prices for goods and services will have already risen. The initial recipients are the state and its clientele of banks and politically connected big companies. The last recipients are wage earners, people on salary, and retirees on fixed incomes. Inflation creates poverty and makes the super-rich, who have a direct connection to the banking system, even richer. The few profit at the expense of the many.

4. Why government money ruins us economically

"What is viewed as bad in an economic downturn are the effects coming into play of the consequences of an artificial boom fueled by credit expansion."

- Ludwig von Mises

You now know how money comes into being — in a good as well as in a bad monetary system — and who profits at the expense of whom. We now want to turn to the question of what structural effects inflation (i.e., an expansion of the money supply) has on an economy. In our discussion we will primarily concentrate on business loans.

Let us forget for a moment as we delve into this that there are banks. Let's go back to our small city. Local fisherman Frank catches ten pounds of fish every day from the large lake near the city. But our fisherman is ambitious. He has noticed that fishing from shore he can only catch a limited number of fish. In the middle of the lake, the fish must be bigger and more plentiful, he reasons. So why not use a fishing boat and attach a large net to it? Instead of ten pounds of fish per day, he might be able to catch 100 pounds per day. The only problem is that he has neither a boat nor a net.

Frank must first look for suitable trees and cut them down, then build the boat and finally he needs to make a fishing net. Frank calculates that he needs six months to make the boat and the fishing net.[7] But what will he eat during that time? If he works full-time on the boat and the net, he cannot at the same time catch his ten pounds of fish every day. Who will feed him, his wife, and his children during those six months? Who will clothe them and buy toys for them while Frank is working to produce his capital goods? Obviously, Frank needs to save up resources before he starts his project. He will need to put aside a part of the ten pounds that he catches every day. He and his family cannot consume the entire ten pounds of fish, or exchange it all for other goods. He will need to save some of it. He must reduce his consumption to something less than the possible maximum and, for example, save five pounds of fish daily for six months. Or — if money has arisen in our small city by the lake — he must put away part of the revenue he earns from selling his daily catch. He must keep saving until he has sufficient reserves to sustain himself and his family during the time it takes for him to build the boat and make the net. He must forgo consumption and put away real savings, represented by either a room full of cured fish, or (in a monetary economy) a bag full of gold coins. After six months of saving, Frank has sufficient savings to start building his boat. If Frank completes his boat and net in the estimated half a year, he can — if his expectations are right — increase his fish production by a factor of ten. Not just he and his family, but the entire town will now be better off. This is because the production of real consumable goods — fish — has risen dramatically.

In fact, the process we just described is the most important form of economic growth. Through an increase in real savings, the production of capital goods is made possible, which in turn allows for greater production of goods and/or the production of higher quality goods. The essential requirement is that sufficient real savings have been set aside first.

What happens if our fisherman saves for six months, but is unable to complete his boat and net in the following six months due to circumstances beyond his control? Then Frank must stop his project prematurely, because he needs to feed his family. It might turn out that all his work was for nothing.

But Frank does not necessarily have to be the one who saves! Others can do this for him. But **someone** has to do it, because Frank's family cannot live on nothing but thin air. Frank can look for an investor who is willing to give him the required credit, whether that is in the form of money or real goods. He can ask friends and acquaintances for a loan. If that does not work, or he does not want to do that, he can look to others for credit by placing an ad in the local newspaper.

What is the basic prerequisite for finding a willing investor? Frank's entrepreneurial plan must be realistic and have a good chance of success; that much is clear.

Two prerequisites must be met before Frank can obtain a loan: a) the money first has to be saved by someone. That means that *someone* must have already forgone consumption. They must have consumed *less* than they earned. And b) both parties, the borrower and the lender, must agree on the interest rate that the borrower will pay for the loan.

If Frank makes his investment plans during a time when people are saving more because of economic insecurity and consequently not a lot is being invested and the demand for loans is low, then the interest rate will tend to be low. But if he goes looking for a loan at a time when many other entrepreneurs are seeking to make investments, then the demand for credit is high and the interest rate for loans will be comparatively higher.

The willingness of individuals to save for the future is referred to as their "time preference rate." It is the variable that expresses how much people are prepared to forgo present consumption in order to increase their future consumption. Societal and institutional developments can influence this willingness to save, this attitude towards the future, in a systematic way. The monetary system can also do so. More on that later.

Every good has its price, determined by supply and demand. The same applies to loans. For loans, present goods (money units today) versus future goods (money units later) are exchanged. This price for money loans is often expressed as a percentage of the amount borrowed, and is called the interest rate. The interest rate reflects the willingness to save, i.e., people's time preference rate. The interest rate shows how ready and willing people are to save and to forgo consumption, and for how long. It thus indirectly shows the quantity of real savings.

There are always desirable investment projects that are not undertaken because there are not enough savings available. The projects simply cannot be carried out because people are not willing to forgo consumption for long enough. Let's assume that the market interest rate in our city is 20%. But Frank only expects a rate of return of 15% on his project. So for Frank, this market interest rate is too high and he will not undertake his project. But if more were saved, the interest rate would fall, let's say, to 10%. Now, Frank's project and many others like it are potentially profitable. New investment projects are begun and can also be successfully brought to conclusion. That is because the real savings, the resources available for investment purposes, have risen. If, on the other hand, less is saved, then the interest rate rises, and fewer projects may be profitably undertaken. For this reason, it is very important that the interest rate is not distorted and manipulated. We will call a non-manipulated interest rate the *natural rate of interest.*

If our fisherman-entrepreneur Frank has found a lender and they have agreed on the conditions for a loan, he can now carry out his investment as planned. And if his expectations as to how many fish he will be able to catch and how much he will be able to sell them for are correct, then he will make a profit. He will pay the lender the agreed-upon interest, and at the end of the loan period he will have paid off his debt.

But if Frank has miscalculated the returns on his investment or his expectations are not fulfilled for reasons that he has no control over, he may have a cash flow problem. If he cannot find a way to resolve that problem by himself, for example by reducing his operating costs, or making use of an inheritance or a loan from someone else, he may well go bankrupt.

What effect will it have on the economy of our city by the lake if Frank goes bankrupt and cannot repay his loan? Well, fisherman Frank will have to make changes. He must get back on his feet financially, and try to find ways to repay the remaining debt that he had before his bankruptcy. Frank had an employee, a young man who helped him construct the boat and who later helped him cast the net, who will now need to find a new job. And certainly, the lender will have to write off as a loss all or part of the loan he gave to Frank.

Has anything else happened? No, no bank needs to be rescued due to Frank going bankrupt, and no politician needs to tell people on TV that "we need to rescue Frank. If Frank goes bankrupt, we will have to pay for that down the road. There is no alternative to rescuing Frank."

Up to this point, as we mentioned at the beginning of our story, no bank has been involved. For a bank that always holds a reserve of 100% of customer deposits at all times, the situation would be almost identical. Only that which had been already saved could then be invested. A bank with a 100% reserve ratio can only issue loans if there are depositors who have agreed to do without their deposited money and forgo consumption for a while.

The bank would merely take on the role of an intermediary between lenders and borrowers. The bank checks out the creditworthiness of the potential borrower and puts its own capital on the line if the borrower turns out to be unable to pay back the loan. The bank makes its profit on the difference between the interest rate charged from borrowers and the interest rate that it pays to the depositors who fund the loans being made.

In this kind of loan issuance, there is no expansion of the money supply. A saver, for example, a hunter working in our imaginary city, who forgoes consumption for a period of time, lends money to the bank, which in turn provides a loan to the fisherman. In essence, the monetary equivalent of real savings is transferred from one person to another.

We now want to look at what happens when banks create new money by extending credit, in that they hold only a part of their customers' deposits as reserves, while offering the rest as loans in the market. For the discussion that follows, it should be noted that this goes for *all* artificial credit expansion funded by money creation.

The expansion of the money supply is more extensive the less reserves banks have to keep on hand to meet potential demands for redemption. If central banks also participate in this "let's print money" game, as is the case in every country today, then the money creation pedal can really hit the metal.

In the current monetary system in which money is no longer linked to anything, an unlimited expansion of the money supply can in theory be carried out at any time. Nevertheless, banks and central banks are "careful." They know that they have to watch out and that they must not overdo their money creation. Ludwig von Mises put it cogently in his work *Human Action*, when he wrote:

> *"If a thing has to be used as a medium of exchange, public opinion must not believe that the quantity of this thing will increase beyond all bounds. Inflation is a policy that cannot last forever."*

Banks and the central banks are walking a tightrope: on the one hand, printing as much money as possible to maximize their own profits; on the other hand only so much that the prices of goods and services do not climb too fast and the purchasing power of money does not decline too fast. Otherwise, people would lose their trust in the money.

> *"In contrast to a healthy monetary system, in a fractional reserve system, loanable funds may enter the market because banks can — given their legally privileged status — create money out of nothing. The bank simply prints a warehouse receipt and loans it to the fisherman, so that the fisherman can finance his investment project. You can see the enormous difference: no one here is forgoing consumption, and none of the depositors have declared to the bank that they would be willing to relinquish control of their deposits for an agreed-upon period of time."*

On the contrary: the depositors wish to retain immediate access to their deposits at all times, in order to be able to buy consumption goods. That is the opposite of forgoing consumption.

No one saved here, and thus no one made the financial means available to sustain the fisherman and his family during the construction of the boat and the making of the net. But the money creation and the warehouse receipt suggest the opposite to the fisherman. He believes that there are enough real resources available to bring his investment project to a successful conclusion.

But what influence does money creation have on the general level of interest rates, in other words, on the price that must be paid for loans? Please consider this: *more* loans can now be offered. Ergo: interest rates will fall due to the money creation, even though this time, *savings did not increase.* They will be lower than the interest rates that would have prevailed in a free market, had money *not* been created out of thin air. The interest rate has been artificially lowered, and this has — at first glance — barely recognizable, but very considerable effects. We can no longer talk about a *natural* rate of interest, instead we must speak of an *artificial* or *manipulated* interest rate.

Put yourself in the position of the fisherman. He needs a loan for his planned investment (the boat and the net). His calculations have shown him that the maximum interest rate that he can afford to pay is 15%. But say the current interest rate is 20%. This means that his investment will not pay off. In a system in which the money supply cannot be expanded by manipulation, he must save money himself or wait until other market participants have saved more money. Then the interest rate will very likely fall. Before that, he cannot start on his project.

But if money is created out of thin air, the same effect occurs as when someone has saved the money: the interest rate falls. The fisherman of course observes the fall in the interest rate, and if he is offered an interest rate of 10%, he takes it. He invests. He thus initiates a project that he otherwise would not have begun if the money first had to be saved, or if the money had not been created out of thin air. Note that he cannot know whether the credit provided to him comes from real savings or out of thin air. After all, he is a fisherman and not a fortune teller.

Have you ever gone on a hike in an area that you don't know and had to rely on a compass? Without any hiking map? No? It actually works very well. The compass needle is a very reliable indicator of which direction you need to go. The same goes for the interest rate as a "compass needle" for entrepreneurial action. But this is only true for the *natural* rate of interest; manipulated interest rates cannot fulfill this function. A rate of interest artificially manipulated downwards is like a compass needle being influenced by a magnet which erroneously signals to investment-ready enterprises that people have saved enough.

And thus *more* investment projects are started than can be successfully completed. The reason: the means of production and resources in the economy are too scarce to cover all projects. Ultimately, the quantity of possible profitable investments is limited by the quantity of real savings. And money created out of thin air does not create any new real resources. If no savings exist, the fisherman cannot feed his family and will have to stop his boat project. He cannot eat the newly printed warehouse receipts.

Ludwig von Mises described this in *Human Action*:

> *"The whole entrepreneurial class is, as it were, in the position of a master-builder whose task it is to erect a building out of a limited supply of building materials. If this man overestimates the quantity of the available materials, he drafts a plan for the execution of which the means at his disposal are not sufficient. He oversizes the groundwork and the foundations and only discovers later in the progress of the construction that he lacks the materials needed for the completion of the structure ... [There occurred] an inappropriate employment of the means at his disposal."*

With this last sentence on the inappropriate employment of resources, Mises indicates a very important point. Resources and means of production are *always* scarce. If there were no scarcity, we would not have to save, we would not have to carry out profitability calculations and we would live in a utopia. Do you think you are living in some kind of utopia? We don't think so either. For that reason, it is important that means of production and resources are allocated to the right uses — to the correct, and most importantly, to the most urgent use at the time. This means that the resources are not wasted and are optimally used. Waste makes us all poorer.

But what happens when new credit, not backed by real savings, finds its way to entrepreneurs throughout the economy? In the beginning, the artificial expansion creates an artificial economic boom; demand increases everywhere … for workers, which raises wages, and for other factors of production, which also increase in price. Prices of consumer goods increase. Why? Because wages have risen and workers can now afford more than before. Entrepreneurs feel that their investment decisions were right — their selling prices are rising, after all. They expand production further.

Other entrepreneurs, who up to now had been holding back, also decide to invest; they now want a piece of the pie as well. The investment plans get more and more daring. Workers are pushed to their physical limits and are working overtime. Their wages continue to climb. The demand for loans increases. Because workers receive a wage increase and the interest rate is so low, they also take on more loans. Some to buy a house, others want a new car, paid for with debt of course. Everything rises: wages, real estate prices, share prices. Everyone is happy. It appears that we can automatically become richer without having to work hard, without doing any saving, and without having to forgo any present consumption. A feverish euphoria spreads. The demand for loans keeps going up, with the effect that interest rates start to rise …

Question: When interest rates start to rise, what happens to investments that were only profitable because the interest rate had been artificially lowered? They become unprofitable. That is clear, right? The boom *must* then come to a halt.

The problem would not exist if the necessary and natural economic correction were allowed to happen. We know that this might at first seem pretty heartless. But shouldn't enterprises that only were profitable due to manipulated interest rates now be allowed to suffer the consequences and go bankrupt? Those enterprises are wasting the scare resources of society. You don't want us all to become poorer, do you?

Do you remember the concept of the "we create money from thin air, and create wealth that way" model of economics? The problem is that it cannot work.

Most politicians do not understand this. And they are at this point enjoying their time in the limelight. They make big speeches about how the economy needs to be jump-started. A lot of investment credit is handed out — created out of thin air of course. Now the state has to intervene, they say: "We have to junk all the old cars that are making our streets unsightly. And everyone will receive money as a reward. Cash for clunkers! Also, those who are going to buy a new refrigerator will be subsidized: we will call that a CO2 abatement reward. And you central bankers, do something, please lower the interest rates so that the bankers can once again hand out cheap credit." Does this sound familiar?

If the interest rates are continually set lower, an economy becomes dependent on cheap money, like a drug addict who can't make it through the day without their regular fix.

After the collapse of Lehman Brothers in September 2008, governments and central banks worldwide immediately set the monetary lever to "rescue mode" with permanently cheap interest rates. All governments, banks, and financial companies that looked like they might go under have been bailed out — whatever it took. Note that we didn't come up with the phrase "whatever it takes." That line comes from the ECB boss "Super Mario" Draghi. In formulating that line, he was referring to saving the euro, when someone asked him about its future.

Believe us: the elite politicians (and by "elite," we are referring to their position, and not to the quality of their work) recognize the coming danger.

They know exactly what is at risk when interest rates climb and the unavoidable correction comes. They are only buying time with their bail-out policies. The situation will not improve. Quite the contrary! But who does it help if politicians buy time? First and foremost, the politicians themselves. They serve one or two terms in office, and then they slide into a safe job as a minister, state secretary, or some other lucrative office, and in the end they will have earned a fat pension for their retirement. A pension so high that *you* have to work your entire life to pay for it.

Don't let yourself be fooled by politicians and their so-called "experts." An economy does not become richer by creating more and more money. First there has to be savings, and then capital and consumer goods can be manufactured. *This is the only way a society can become richer.*

Let's look at exactly what the unavoidable correction looks like to this "money out of thin air" scheme.

Interest rates rise. Costs skyrocket upwards, as do wages, because companies have taken on projects wildly, and have hired lots of workers. Think of our fisherman. Suddenly the cost of wood for his boat has risen, his assistant wants more money or he will leave for a better-paying job, and paying for food and other necessities for his family is getting more and more expensive. That is because the prices of consumer goods are increasing, because workers and employees have more money and because consumer goods production has fallen a bit. Our fisherman no longer fishes, but is working on his boat. During the time he is working on it, fish production falls and the price of fish climbs unless more has been saved. But this was not the case here. Fish has not been cured and stored beforehand to be sold in the market. The only thing that was produced was more money. People are not willing to wait until the boat is ready. They want more fish *now.* Pressure on the fisherman increases. Interest rates and costs are strangling him financially. At the same time, he sees that he can now earn good profits by just fishing from the shore. He ultimately stops his project. His boat and net are unfinished, so the resources he has used go to waste. Society's scarce savings have been wasted.

In the same way, the artificial boom breaks down and turns into a bust in our economy today. The rising interest rates lead to a situation in which additional credit for new investments is only provided very hesitantly, the bust intensifies, and economic growth collapses. In addition — and this is very important — it becomes clear that a lot of investments had been identified as profitable only because interest rates were artificially low, but they no longer are, because the interest rates have risen. Companies have to cut back or go bankrupt. Workers lose their jobs, and those who are able to remain on the payroll have to accept pay cuts. Consumption falls drastically. Prices look like they will fall. Loans provided in the boom can no longer be paid back. This in turn has as a logical result that the money quantity that was expanded by issuing these loans now threatens to shrink.

The bottom line: Banks have to write off claims, which tears ugly holes in their balance sheets, which then have to be filled by taxes that *you* have to pay. This is done in such a skillful manner that you don't notice it, at least not at first. Or new debt is run up. And you won't notice that at first, either, but at some point, when your money buys less, you will. You definitely notice it when your net paycheck or pension no longer stretches to cover your household budget.

The economic correction that occurs should be viewed positively. After all, it ends a sham boom and corrects it. Scarce resources are finally allocated to their most efficient use and are no longer misused in unprofitable projects. Even if the income of some workers falls during the correction, when looked at correctly, that is not a problem. After all, when demand falls, the prices of consumer goods will also fall and people can buy more for less money.

But wait … We have not taken the central bank into account. The experts who work there are very sensitive to falling prices! They will lower the interest rates *again*, the banking system will be supplied *yet again* with *even more* liquidity and the business of credit expansion will ramp up again, to prevent prices from falling.

But why is the economic recession not allowed to happen and prices not allowed to fall? Very simple. Because falling prices in a pure paper money system would trigger a so-called deflationary spiral, which would reveal as unprofitable investment projects that were only started as a result of the artificial credit expansion. And because we have lived through many such ups and downs in the past decades, a huge number of unprofitable investments would come to light, with unforeseeable consequences. All those highly indebted companies and people would now have huge problems, because when prices fall, it is harder to pay back debts. Individuals and companies with a lot of debt would have to go bankrupt in droves. Not to speak of the biggest debtor in the economy: the state. And if the debtors are no longer paying their debts, the banking system will ultimately collapse.

Politicians would have a hard time explaining all of this, and politicians would be run out of office. And what would happen then, what would be the worst effect? Because the vast majority of people do not know that the boom was triggered by money created out of thin air, *the politicians* will now be called on to act!

This is a vicious circle. It gives one pause to consider that most people are robbed by inflation. The following comparison applies to this call for help: someone breaks into your house at night and the person who broke in is the same person you call on for help in finding the burglar. You just are not aware that they are the same person.

Every artificial boom *must* be followed by an economic bust. The bust exposes the damage from the misallocated investments from the boom. The partially completed fishing boat reveals misallocated resources. Those resources have been wasted and are not available for other projects. The quantity of capital goods — which determines the productive capacity of an economy — has been reduced (relative to what it could have been). We have become poorer as a society.

The insidious thing about these artificially created booms and busts and bail-out orgies are the changes and shifts that they cause in the income and wealth structure of a society. These are irreversible. Purchasing power and assets shift — the tendency is from the bottom to the top. A few profit at the expense of the many. The trend is for the rich to get richer and the poor poorer. We already described the effects of inflation in the previous chapter, in detail.

Upon closer inspection, we must conclude that our present monetary system is inherently destructive. Interest rates have to be continually lowered to prevent the exposure of the misallocation of resources that was covered up by prior booms. You may ask yourself what happens if the central bank never allowed interest rates to rise, but lowered them at the slightest sign of a crisis, or maintained them at a rate close to zero. Wouldn't that prevent the economic correction and allow the boom to continue without interruption? Wouldn't it help our fisherman if he could obtain credit at a zero interest rate? Wouldn't it prevent the deflationary spiral?

Perhaps he could keep himself above water a bit longer with help from the low or zero interest rate, and stick with his project against the wishes of the consumers who would prefer not to wait any longer to eat fish. However, due to the money production and the "free" interest rates, his costs will continue to rise, faster and faster. Zero interest rates do not magically produce goods. Rather, they lead to new bubbles and additional malinvestment. At most, what artificially low interest rates can do is postpone the inevitable, inasmuch as the fisherman is pulling economic resources away from other worthwhile projects. We cannot get around the fact that too many big projects were started and that not enough real resources are available to finish them all.

Continually creating new money with zero interest rates is not a solution to the misuse of resources. And if the situation continues, in the end, so much money will have been produced, so much debt will be in the system that people will lose their trust in the money, and our current *bad money* will become useless as a means of exchange. The deflationary spiral has been prevented at the cost of hyperinflation. But maybe the politicians will head this off ahead of time and reduce over-indebtedness in some other way. The other possibilities, such as a debt "haircut," currency reform, or a wealth tax are very painful. More on that in Chapter 8.

The highly likely resulting loss of confidence and trust in the money is completely ignored by so-called economic experts. Does the following line ring a bell? "We foresee a slight economic recovery, and we see no threat of inflation at this time."

What will you do when you see that the purchasing power of your money has fallen and is likely to go down further? You will attempt to get rid of it, right? Just like millions and millions of others. Probably all at the same time. And what happens when demand for money collapses in this way and demand for real goods explodes?

Prices will rise, faster than most people can imagine. And what do central banks have to do when the prices rise — after all, it is their job to keep prices stable, right? They cut back on money production and raise interest rates. And now the question comes: Can interest rates be raised in a monetary system in which there is more debt than ever?

Instead of us providing an answer, we turn to Ludwig von Mises again. You will see that there is in fact economic literature available that explains the problems created by printing money. The following comes from an essay Mises wrote in 1931:

> *"Sooner or later, it must become evident that the economic boom turns out to have been built on sand. Because sooner or later, credit expansion through the creation of additional money must come to a standstill. The banks could be forced, either because they wanted to or because of strong pressure from outside, to not carry this policy on forever. The advancing increase of the money supply leads to advancing price increases. But inflation can only continue so long as the opinion exists that it will stop in the foreseeable future. But if the view wins out that inflation will not end, then panic breaks out. The public already takes into account the future price increases in its view of money and goods, so that the prices leap excessively, and as the use of this money compromised by monetary expansion falls, people flee into foreign money, to precious metals, to tangible assets, eventually to barter; in short, the currency collapses."*

The Austrian school economists in the first half of the 20th century, primarily Ludwig von Mises, described the processes that are triggered when credit is expanded. One of Mises's students, Friedrich A. von Hayek, won the Nobel Prize in economics in 1974 for his Austrian monetary and business cycle theory.

You may now with justification ask yourself why someone who won such an important prize has been mostly ignored by governments and decision-makers and why he continues to be ignored. We will return to this question in Chapter 9.

Summary:

Money creation through credit expansion leads to fake and unsupportable economic booms. Investments are undertaken that only appear profitable because money is created out of thin air and the interest rate is artificially lowered. But real resources are insufficient to successfully bring those investments to completion. Sooner or later, cost increases and higher interest rates expose these malinvestments. Unfortunately the subsequent unavoidable and wholly necessary economic correction is politically unpopular, and is fought with additional interest rate cuts. Society becomes poorer as a result of the resulting malinvestments. Capital goods lose value, valuable time is lost, and unemployment increases. The monetary expansion causes redistribution of income and wealth within society — as a rule, from the bottom income classes to those at the top. The rich become richer and the poor get poorer. The core of the destruction should be attributed to the paper money system. If the policy of interest rate cuts and ever stronger monetary expansion continues, people eventually lose trust in the money. At the end of this path is the unavoidable hyperinflation and a collapse of the monetary system.

5. How the state exploits you with inflation

"Thanks to the unlimited power of the central bank to print money, states are able to amass ever greater mountains of debt. They are able to wage hot and cold wars that they would otherwise be unable to finance. And they can start an unending number of projects and throw themselves into adventures that otherwise would be unthinkable."

- Hans Hermann Hoppe

If you look at politics worldwide, you get the impression that there is only one goal in this game: *power*. Whoever is in power wants to remain there, and all that everyone else strives for is to get there. The late German economist Roland Baader said to one of the authors in 2012: *"There are two ways to exercise power. Power through the sword and power through bread and circuses, which in the modern version is called the welfare state."*

Imagine that you are the state. You have a monopoly on the use of force and you are the ultimate judge in all conflicts. You can rule in your own favor if you want. You can use this power to compel or regulate or prohibit certain behaviors. You can raise taxes.

You can also take the property of others without compensation. It is almost like having Tolkien's ring. A nice position to be in!

In your quest for unlimited power, at first you try to consolidate your power. You bring strategically important sectors under your control: police, justice, military, communication, transport, energy, the media, and — most of all — the education sector.

Because your subjects far outnumber you, you need at least their tacit support. You need to invent some story to legitimize your authority, because the use of force to maintain your privileged position will not work over the long term.

Maybe you invent the notion of "the divine right of kings" and establish a monarchy, or maybe you float the idea of "people's sovereignty" and give access to the state apparatus to all classes in society.

You want to make various groups dependent on you to ensure their support. You grant privileges, subsidies, and simple transfers to buy and keep popular support. The more public servants you have indebted to you, the better. You can be assured of their support because they get their income from you. They are not likely to bite the hand that feeds them! Other means of strengthening your power are control over the public pension systems, health care systems, and social transfer systems. These systems displace private welfare assistance and neighborly support. They create dependency and weaken competing "natural" institutions such as the family, which traditionally help in times of need.

So far so good. But there is a catch. Maintaining power is very expensive! Subsidies, public servants, welfare transfers — these all cost money.

How to pay for this power? People are seldom happy about paying taxes. Taxes show that the good deeds of the state are not really free. The support of many has been bought and paid for by promises and graft, but what about the others, those not on the payroll? Many of them become enemies or opponents, especially those you tax to pay for it.

If only there was a way to finance state expenditures without raising taxes! A way to make citizens pay without them realizing it. A system to allow money and wealth to be extracted from the citizens without them being aware of it, and so convoluted and complex that only a few could understand it.

As it happens, there is such a system. In its most pernicious form, it is our current paper money system. The monetary system is a sector of the economy which is of strategic importance to the state, and one it has interfered in from the very beginning. We turn to Roland Baader again:

> *"In any case, the state needs huge quantities of money to exercise its authority. Because the required amounts have risen to such astronomical heights, taxes are no longer sufficient. Everywhere around the world, the state has therefore monopolized the printing of money in order to create gigantic sums of money out of thin air."*

Think about it. If you control the money supply, then you can finance your expenses not through unpopular taxes, but simply by producing more money. You print the money! Just like a counterfeiter, but legally. *You* make the rules, so you can do this as much as you like.

Prices rise and the citizens pay for this in the form of a loss of purchasing power, because their money is becoming worth less and less. Remember the redistribution of purchasing power that we discussed in Chapter 3: the state, as the first recipient of money, gains at the cost of the people. But the people do not see the connection between the state monopoly on money production and things becoming more expensive. There are of course many other factors that can influence prices. You can easily make one of those other factors the scapegoat for the rising price level. Greedy speculators or rich CEOs, for example. Or some natural catastrophe. Or an oil crisis.

It also does not have to be an *absolute* loss of purchasing power. The reason is that the growth in productivity puts a brake on things getting more expensive and conceals the effects of money creation. Without a steady stream of new money, prices would have been falling. Instead they merely stagnate and remain flat, thanks to the state's tireless money production. So we have only a *relative* loss of purchasing power, compared to the situation without the increased money supply.

You can also set up a complicated financial system that no one can understand. Then you don't have to use the obvious and unsophisticated process of printing money yourself; instead you can produce brightly colored pieces of paper on which you print the words "Treasury bond."

Your friendly bankers buy these securities and keep them at the central bank, which has the money-creation monopoly you gave it and is your officially designated "independent" central bank. In return for selling or pledging the government bonds to the central bank, the banks get fresh, newly created money. Ultimately, your debt is financed by new money production — and the traces are covered up … and that is genius.

In short, you — as the state — exploit the fact that people understand the connection between state expenditures and taxes, but they do not understand the connection between state expenditures and money production and its main effect: price inflation. In this way the monetary monopoly is able to conceal the costs of war, of welfare state programs, and of prestige projects such as Germany's "energy switch" (in which nuclear power was phased out in favor of wind and solar power, subsidized by the state) and it hides the effects of policies that people would otherwise not support. The money monopoly is an arm of the state monopoly, and should be vigorously challenged and resisted by every citizen.

But now we put the delusions of power aside and return to reality. You are not the state. You unfortunately are on the other end. You are *merely* a citizen and cannot create a money monopoly, but you have to live with the fact that we have one.

It is now understandable why the state has such a great interest in getting away from gold. In a state paper money system, going into debt is as easy as pie for the state. Recall that loans are created out of nothing. And the state is in control of this never-ending source of money. That is the main reason why the state has no problem going into debt.

Another reason for them to keep us away from gold is the apparent safety that state debt (government bonds) offers to investors — who are mostly, whether directly or indirectly, individuals. *Not me,* you might think now, *I will not loan money to those crooks, absolutely not!* But you are doing just that. If you have life insurance or a private pension plan, then … welcome to the club. You are then also a financier of politics, the same politics of waste that angers you nightly on the news. Your indirect investment in government bonds through life insurance and financial assets represents an additional advantage of state financing through debt instead of financing through taxes. If people are taxed, they feel poorer. But going into debt means that bonds are issued which then end up in someone's portfolio, and that person feels richer. That is an illusion, however. In both cases — taxes and debt — resources are taken out of the productive private sector and pumped into the wasteful government sector.

In both instances, the private sector becomes poorer and the state becomes richer.

Of course, no one can really imagine that a state could go bankrupt. In practice, that is also hard to conceive of. After all, there is the central bank, which would take over the state's debt and would bail out the government, at *your* cost, of course. The value of money is destroyed faster when the central bank has to print virtually unlimited quantities to bail out the government.

While the Fed can freely buy government bonds, the ECB cannot. The ECB is indeed forbidden from buying up government debt, but there are enough possibilities for it to ultimately take over state financing, working together with the banking system which is tightly allied to the state. As we have already described, banks can pledge government bonds that they have acquired as collateral at the central bank in order to obtain *fresh* money. *Fresh* here means *new* money. Money that did not exist the moment before that transaction occurred.

The biggest item in most national budgets is expenditures for "social security, unemployment and labor" or simply put, the welfare state. This also explains why those in power would rather take the path of debt than to raise taxes. This is because first taking the money from the citizens in the form of taxes and then immediately returning it to them in the form of welfare payments would be far too easy to understand. It would be easy for the taxpayer to see how much money the Moloch, the state, uses for itself and how much of it goes to waste. Pretty clear, isn't it?

What is clear is that our current welfare state or "unfair state," given its real social effects, could not be financed just from taxes.

It is not an accident that this "unfair state" and its cancer-like growth has gone hand in hand with the end of the gold standard and the transition to a paper money system. The modern unfair state has survived by the accumulation of a gigantic public debt made possible by the paper money system. If it had been financed by taxes alone, the people would have revolted long ago.

Let's take a look at the total debt of the German government as of November 2013. It comes to about two trillion euros: €2,000,000,000,000. Yet this figure looks modest compared to the debt figure for the United States. In 2013, the Federal government was

$17 trillion in the red. And governments worldwide can't even make do with the taxes they bring in! They shamelessly keep running up more and more debt. The temptation is just too great to hand out electoral gifts in the form of debt-financed election goodies in return for votes in order to get elected or to stay in office. Wilhelm Busch's line comes to mind: *Once one's reputation is ruined, life is free and easy.*

When government debt comes due, the state is well behaved and pays it back. But never out of taxes they have collected. That is because for a state, *repayment* does not mean the same as when normal people use the term. When *you* have paid back your debt, then your loan balance is zero. When the state pays back its debt, then generally, it does so by taking on *new* debt. And because our money is worth less and less, it is easy for the state to do this, thanks to its own inflationary monetary policy.

The creditors — those who loaned the money — are hurt, but the mega-debtors profit. If only we citizens could make use of a system that is so profitable! But in monetary affairs, the state does not allow any competition. It will not share its money monopoly with anyone. And few dare question this monopoly. Maybe this book will help to change that. Help us with this task. Talk to family, with friends, in clubs, at church, or at your local bar. Help enlighten people to open their eyes. It is incredible how much depends on this. It is worth it. Do it for your children and grandchildren.

Back to the topic at hand. Critics will object and say that the state also pays interest on its debt. Doesn't the state have to raise taxes at least for the interest payment? That is another misconception. The state can just issue new state debt (bonds) to raise the money to pay for its interest payments. Neither the debt nor the interest needs to be paid for out of taxes, but can be paid for by taking on new debt, meaning, creating more money.

In order to keep the enormous interest rate payments within limits, states normally manipulate expectations with regard to price inflation. This is because there is a premium already baked into the market interest rate to cover the expected loss of money′s purchasing power. The higher the expected loss of purchasing power, the higher the interest rate a creditor will demand.

If the state as debtor is successful in keeping the expectations with regard to money devaluation low, it saves a lot of money and/or it does not have to print as much new money in order to pay its debt. That is because the loan rate that it has to pay will be lower.

But how does the state lower expectations about money devaluation?

When you have sufficient money, it is quite easy. You hire a large number of employees and let them work for you, based on the motto: "Don't trust any statistic that you have not falsified yourself."

For that purpose, the German government at some point entrusted this task to the Federal Statistics Office (*Statistisches Bundesamt*). It still does. 2,940 people worked there as of 2013. Month after month, they prepare all kinds of statistics that no one really needs. But the Federal Statistics Office publishes a monthly rate of price increases, also called the inflation rate, which is calculated from the consumer price index. In the U.S., the Bureau of Labor Statistics is the main statistics office with the mind-boggling budget of $632.7 million for 2016. All for producing useless statistics.

The rate of price increase (the inflation rate) is probably the most difficult economic figure to understand for the non-economist. In all probability, the statisticians at the Office — working for the state — make it so complex that no layman has the faintest chance of understanding what the figures mean. And if people now and then express doubts about the official figures, then the experts hem and haw, saying it is all imaginary, and has to do with "perceived inflation." Wow, we citizens must be dumb. We are not "perceiving" inflation correctly.

In stating the official rate of increase in the price level — we do not want to use the term price inflation — the German Federal Statistics Office has one purpose in mind: that the continual loss of value of our money must be concealed and a loss of trust in the state money must be prevented. A paper money system is based on trust. If trust is lost, no one wants to hold the paper anymore, prices explode, and the system collapses. Weimar, Germany in the year 1923 comes to mind. The state obviously does not want that. The state wants to continue to profit from its control of the monetary system.

Manipulating expected price increases downward is one of its most clever parlor tricks.

In calculating the rate of price increase, the statisticians use a kind of virtual basket of goods. Everything is put into this basket that you and your family usually need to live: rent or mortgage payments, food, toiletries, a car, etc. Now estimate for yourself the percentage that you have to pay out of your wages or salary for food, electricity, and other essentials. Does your result match the official figures?

At the end of 2013 in Germany, food was weighted at 10.3% and electricity at 2.6% in the statistical basket of goods. Was your figure higher? What were you thinking? Why do you eat so much? And why do you leave your lights on for so long? Think of the environment, go to bed earlier, or light a candle; that works too and is even more romantic! More romantic at least than the cold light of the new energy-saving light bulbs mandated by Brussels and Washington. In addition, you can save a lot of money and spend more for other items like wax candles. Pretty cynical, right? But you don't behave as the statisticians assume.

For a family of four with a monthly income of 3,000 euros (about $3,250), these figures mean that food and electricity together cost about 390 euros. But both food and energy in Germany have become considerably more expensive in the past few years. You may want to compare this budget with your own figures!

And we won't even discuss what the result would be for a single retired elderly woman with a monthly income of 800 euros ($880).

The fact is that the weighting of food and energy — a large portion of the average family's income — is clearly set too low. And for lower incomes, the incorrect weighting is even more crucial.

We absolutely have to explain to you *the hedonic methods* used in official price statistics. Sounds complicated? It isn't. It means for example that if the new PC that you just bought, which is twice as powerful as your four-year old computer, cost the same, then the statisticians use a *lower* price when they count it. The statisticians tabulate their charts and graphs as if the price has actually fallen! They explain this as follows: *It is necessary to quantify qualitative improvements of products and to remove them from the price development statistics.* But the problem is that the price did not actually fall. You can't even buy a PC today with the low performance of your old computer. The reduction in price, magically created, which is used to compensate in the price index for price increases in other areas such as food and energy, does not exist in real life.

In the U.S., they use yet another trick to suppress the official rate of price inflation. They call it a correction for the "substitution bias." The reasoning is as follows. If butter rises in price by 100%, but margarine goes up by only 10%, people will reduce their consumption of butter and increase their consumption of margarine. As a consequence, statisticians change the consumer price basket they use to calculate the rate of price inflation. They reduce the weight of butter in their calculations and increase the weight of margarine. In other words, they throw out the goods that rise in price and increase the weight of goods whose price rises more slowly or not at all. The economic reasoning is correct. People would substitute margarine for butter at the margin. But this does not change the fact that butter prices have doubled and that statisticians are manipulating the rate of price inflation downward by changing the weights of the goods in their basket.

Decreasing the weight of fast-rising goods, calculating fast-increasing components of the basket at too low a price and miscalculating using virtual non-existent reductions in prices? One must admit, this clearly seems intentional.

If you want, take a closer look at the website of the German Federal Statistical Office (*www.destatis.de*), particularly the "Prices" section. (If you want to see the official U.S. version, go to the Bureau of Labor Statistics at *http://www.bls.gov/cpi/*). We think that it takes a lot of gumption to use such irrational and complex calculation methods for the topic of consumer prices, and to turn this subject into something that cannot be understood by the average person.

The official price statistics play an essential role in misleading people about the actual loss of purchasing power of their money and how their wealth is expropriated again and again.

Remember in Chapter 3, where we described how technological innovation and the international division of labor over the past several years should have resulted in falling prices? Why is the possibility of falling prices not discussed by economists? Does that not make you suspicious?

What do you think? If the losses of purchasing power that buyers of government bonds could expect were clear to everyone, what rates of interest would the government have to pay for borrowed funds? We cannot tell you exactly. But that is not the point. One thing we can say for sure is this:

If the state (the government, the Bureau of Labor Statistics, etc.) did not hold the official rate of price increases low, the interest rate that the state would have to pay to its creditors to compensate for the loss of money's purchasing power **would be higher** than the low interest rates that it currently pays, all because the state provides us with this fairy tale of stable money.

It is important to note at this time that asset markets, such as the stock market, the bond market, and the real estate market, are *not* included in these price statistics.

And it was here in these sectors that prices increased the most in the past several years. But the official rate of price increases totally ignores that. The experts refer to "asset price inflation," when, for example, the prices of shares of stock as an asset class are driven upwards by monetary expansion.

Price increases in asset markets are also an important factor that has divided society into poor and rich, and continues to do so. If a family can barely live on its income, then there is no money left to invest in the stock market, never mind buying your own home, or rental real estate. And if a normal family is able to save a few dollars for the future, they cannot afford to expose themselves to the swings in value that one must expect when one invests in the financial markets.

On the other hand, those who already have profited from the price increases in the asset markets, become richer and richer and they can use their assets as collateral to take on more loans with which to buy more shares and more real estate.

We have already seen that governments really like financing their state expenditures through monetary production, with the so-called inflation tax, because people feel this is less painful than direct taxes. And people are also (at least until they have read this book) usually unable to figure out the causes.

But financing debt and expenditures through monetary expansion is also attractive to the state for another reason; taxes collected rise as a result of our progressive income tax in direct relation to rising prices for goods and services. A separate book could be written about taxes, but at this point, a short discussion will suffice.

When the tax receipts of the state are greater than in previous years, reports in the press are vastly different than if they were reporting on a company announcing and bragging about its own record profits. There is a big difference. People go to companies voluntarily to obtain the company's products. Companies can only make a profit by making attractive products that people want to buy. If they are not successful in doing so, no one buys their products and they (the products, and possibly the companies) disappear from the market. A record profit is thus a sign of a highly attractive and sought after product, and is also a reason for society as a whole to celebrate. In contrast, people do not pay taxes voluntarily! As Murray Rothbard wrote in his book *For a New Liberty*, "*anyone who promotes the view that taxes should be considered as voluntary payments are welcome to see what happens if they should choose not to pay them.*"

The state has no competition from anyone internally. Within its own borders, the state has the monopoly on the legitimate use of force. That is bad enough. But in the case of increased tax receipts state employees should not then boast about it — they have not produced anything. They have not created new products or created any value.

It would be like a pickpocket bragging about his success in picking pockets, in front of those he robbed. And they are supposed to applaud him for it? The thing that makes a pickpocket a bit sympathetic is that at least he disappears after having robbed you. You no longer see him — if you even saw him at all in the first place. The pickpocket knows that he did wrong. You do not have to be insulted and lectured by him. The state is different. The state does not disappear. It is always there. Raking in taxes year in and year out. But the worst thing about it is that the state does not retreat in shame like the pickpocket. No. The state proudly admits that it robbed you, but claims that it was for your own good! You are supposed to be grateful to the state and celebrate its record tax receipts …

The state bureaucrats are only innovative in one area: how many different ways they can get their hands on your hard-earned money. They do not practice restraint and no area is off-limits, as seen with the taxes on oil and energy and the value-added and sales taxes, to mention a couple. What an idea: a tax on a tax. That is more than chutzpah, and is deceitful at the same time; medieval barons had nothing on our state tax authorities. The old feudal barons would turn green with envy if they could see what tricks are used today to maximize tax collections. Back then, they were honest and upfront about it: your money or your life!

Workers and companies produce things. In competition with other workers and companies, they are the ones who create value. Companies are always striving to meet the wishes of their customers, with the help of their employees. They are striving to bring better products at lower prices to their customers, in competition with other companies, who are doing the same. It is these companies and employees and workers who have their income taken through taxes. Now back to the topic of how monetary expansion and taxes are linked.

Let's begin with an indirect tax, the so-called value-added tax. For every item you purchase (in many countries in Europe), it is already included in the price as a % markup on the item. So it is easy to predict what happens when prices rise due to money creation. Naturally: state income from value-added taxes also rises.

According to the German Federal Statistics Office, income from the value-added tax for the year 2012 was about 142 billion euros.

Ten years earlier, the receipts were "only" 105 billion euros. That is an increase of 35%. Did *your* income rise by 35% in the same period?

Taxes do not just rise automatically, with the progressive income tax they also rise over-proportionally. Following wage increases to compensate for inflation, the state silently and quietly steals an ever bigger portion of the cake that others have baked. This effect is made worse through "bracket creep," when the state does not adjust the income brackets for inflation. It is nothing other than an added tax burden because you have to pay the so-called marginal tax rate for each additionally earned dollar; for every wage or salary increase you get, your tax burden also rises. And you get your annual wage increase, to compensate for the fact that everything has become more expensive, right? Higher prices follow higher wages. Over-proportionally, higher taxes follow higher wages. So why don't our politicians automatically adjust the tax tables in step with the official rate of price increases? Because that would reduce government revenue.

According to a report by tax consultant Dr. Hans-Georg Jatzek in *Der Hauptstadtbrief* (*Letter from Berlin*, Edition 119), a single person in 1960 would have to earn 60,000 euros gross income to be in the German top income tax bracket. Today it is only 55,000 euros. Imagine what an amount 60,000 euros (or about $66,000) would be in today's money! Taking into account the average income, the exploitation of the citizen becomes much clearer: If in 1960, an employee had to earn 20 times the average wage to be in the top income tax bracket, today anyone making about twice the average wage is in that category. That is incredible. Ask your local political representative in your voting district why that is. The answers would interest us. Please send us their responses.

Thanks to these thieving machinations of the past 30 years, the German tax receipts for federal, state, and city levels have gone up from 190 billion to 600 billion euros in the year 2012. The Internet page of the German Federal Finance Ministry says as much.

Arguments as to why that is are given to us in spades: *The state has social responsibilities to fulfill.* Just like the poor pickpocket who says he has hungry children to feed. That is just meaningless babble and empty excuses. The fact is: the state, through inflation and debt, gobbles up more and more resources and assigns more and more tasks to itself.

Imagine if as of today the money supply was frozen, with no further increases. Leaving aside the fact that our money-addicted junkie-economy would immediately collapse, from that moment on, rising prices would no longer be expected. At least, price increases triggered by money creation would no longer automatically lead to higher tax revenues. The interest rates that are continually held low by constant money production would shoot up. The state would no longer be able to cover the tasks it assigns itself through money creation, and would collapse in a state of over-indebtedness. The flow of money through the state's coffers could no longer be sustained.

Given that there appears to be a plan behind what has been described, the question we must ask is *what* plan is being followed. Can it be that politics creates the apparent justification for its own existence? Everyone of course needs a reason for doing what they do. When a person goes to work and is productive, when a company manufactures products or offers services that are bought by customers, then the justification for their activities is apparent. But who needs a politician, and particular why do we need so many of them? And who would need politicians if they did not have money at their disposal to throw around? Imagine if we took their money away. What would they be left with?

The state tends to make the poor poorer and the rich richer by means of its monetary system and its monetary expansion and ever-increasing debt. But because almost no one recognizes this, the state gets away with blaming others. It appears as a kind of nanny and starts to redistribute income. It supposedly takes from the rich and gives to the poor. Quite nice, right? This is the state's own reason for existing, the one that it has assigned itself. It pretends to solve the problems that would not even exist if the state did not have a monopoly on money creation.

It is not just the people who become ever more dependent on state benefits, companies also do. Some do so thorough social transfer payments and the others from all kinds of subsidies. About half of the gross domestic product (GDP) of most industrial economies flows through the hands of the state. The state has become a huge redistribution machine and an important patron that creates ever greater dependency.

How *an ever-growing state* affects the freedom of the individual person is a subject that we will turn to in Chapter 7. But it is apparent that the effects are not good.

The idea that we could take control of the monetary system back from the state ought to make people excited. But who do most people turn to when they get into financial trouble? Exactly. The state. That is a state of affairs the state has created with its *bad money*. It has created dependency in people and in companies. Dependency on social transfers, state projects, state subsidies, and other monetary transfers. The state has corrupted people.

Economist Thorsten Polleit, president of the German Ludwig von Mises Institute, has come up with the term "collective corruption" to describe this phenomenon. A result of collective corruption is that a big part of the population increasingly supports what the state does, although many feel that the limitless monetary expansion and the debt that results from it will not have a happy ending. People remain silent and accept it. They accept that zombie banks and troubled governments are bailed out with money injections from central banks. They accept it out of fear for their own wealth and position. The reason is, if banks, insurers, and over-indebted companies were to really go bankrupt, many savers would suffer losses, and others would lose their jobs, at least over the short term. So they think it is better to do as before, shut their eyes and let the state print more and more money. Many suppress the thought that in the long run they are digging their own graves with this mentality.

Creating dependency generates power. Power over those who are dependent. The circle closes. The fear of many that state money might no longer flow so freely as before gives the state, the government, and other political power-holders unprecedented power. They have not earned this position of power honestly, rather they have created it without justification through the use of *bad money*. They use state money to their own advantage and to bolster their own position.

Summary:

In order to be able to fund ever-increasing state expenditures, primarily to finance the welfare state, governments prefer taking on debt over raising taxes. In this way, the burden on the people is not directly felt. The connections between state debt and its results — redistribution of income and wealth as well as a reduction in the purchasing power of money — are thus skillfully veiled. It now becomes clear why politicians love paper money so much, and cling to it for all they are worth. It is because state debt at current levels is only possible in a state-monopolized paper money system.

Using the consumer price index determined by the State Statistical Office, price stability is simulated, but it does not exist in reality. This has the purpose of maintaining trust in state money and to ensure the flow of loans to the government on the most favorable terms. Potential falls in prices are prevented through expansion of the money supply.

The expansion of the money supply leads to rising prices, to increasing company profits, and to increasing wages and salaries for workers and employees. This raises the state's income from taxes automatically. Progressive taxes mean that more financial means are available to the state than would be the case without an increase of the general price level. At the same time, the rise in prices devalues the state debt that is already accumulated, to the detriment of savers and the users of money.

State money and inflation have created an unstable and corrupt financial system that more and more people are dependent on. And the only one who can bail out companies or people during the always recurring crisis, is the state itself. Thanks to ever-increasing state expenditures people depend ever more on the state. The power of the state increasingly grows and solidifies. People are corrupted by bad money, accept the continual printing of money due to fear for their own wealth, and close their eyes to the unavoidable catastrophe ahead.

6. What inflation does to people

"People burdened by debt at some point take on the habit of turning to others for help instead of turning into an economic and moral anchor for their family and for the wider society."

- Jörg Guido Hülsmann

We don't know how old you are but if you are no longer young, then you probably remember how it was "back then." Perhaps you pine for "the good old days." You have probably told your children or grandchildren how good things were in the good old days. But what exactly was it that was so good back then? Compared to those days, we have everything in abundance now!

What starts as a feeling turns out to be reality, when looked at more closely. Life has become more hectic, don't you think? And that applies to *all* of life: family *and* career. Combining family and career gets harder and harder. Work pressure increases more and more and the family often gets short-changed.

There are more and more divorces. There are more and more single mothers. And why is that? What are the hidden causes of such problems in our society? It seems that society has adopted more of a short-term throw-away consumer attitude. Many questions arise. But you might now skeptically object, saying: "You don't really want to suggest that all these problems are related to the monetary system, do you? That is outrageous!" Let us explain before you close the book in exasperation …

Let's return to our small imaginary city by the lake. There, everything is still going well. The monetary system is a competitive, private money system; the king does not meddle with it. People use gold and silver coins as a means of payment or use warehouse receipts in their stead. This all works great, as before.

And the king rarely gets involved in the life of his subjects. The few taxes that he demands go to maintain a small army that protects the property of his citizens from attack from foreign kings or marauders. The people in his city live in safety, think in a future-oriented manner, and save a lot. Citizens tend to save money first for things that they will need later. When someone needs a loan, the money for that loan must have already been saved by someone else who had forgone consumption. But taking on debt is only done in exceptional cases and emergencies.

Following in the footsteps of his ancestors, our fisherman also behaves this way, heading up a profitable family enterprise. The idea would never enter his mind to borrow money to buy a television or take a vacation trip. And why would he? Everything has a tendency to get cheaper over time.

The fisherman has also never taken out loans to run his family business. He always paid for investments out of retained earnings. Once, when he wanted to buy a bigger boat, he sold shares of his boat to investors, who had previously saved. Why burden yourself with debts unnecessarily when prices are falling so that repayment will be more difficult?

Most people in the city operate under the "first save, then buy" strategy for both small and big purchases. And that includes purchasing a house or a condominium. This is easy to understand, because prices in the city tend to fall over the long term. Conversely, this means that the purchasing power of money in the city continually rises. This happens because the production of goods is always increasing and the money supply increases more slowly, given the pace at which new gold or silver can be dug up. Because goods prices do not rise, it does not make sense to burden yourself unnecessarily with debt. Things are not "running away," as it were. Everything is loose and relaxed. Anyone who has patience is rewarded with falling prices. Saving is very easy and uncomplicated. You need not be a stock market genius to become wealthy; just save cash, which gains more and more in value over the long term.

Our fisherman has buried a sack of gold coins in his cellar for his retirement and for his heirs. A gold coin that will buy a good suit today will still do so in 50 years. And it will most likely pay for a nice shirt and tie to go with it as well.

The general stability and reliability of the economic environment influence people's personalities and the way they plan their lives. Long-term planning pays off. Above all, saving pays off. People share a healthy faith in God and a relaxed attitude to life.

Entrepreneurs in our city finance their projects mainly from their own capital (equity). They are conservative and careful with money. Debt is avoided. People understand that too much debt takes away choices and restricts opportunities, so low debt levels are important. It allows them to be independent and flexible. Our fisherman does not need to take out a mortgage. After saving for ten years, he buys a house for himself and his family, with his own money. He does not have business debt. He acts independently. He can even take a vacation when he wants to. He does not have to labor at jobs he does not want to do in order to pay off a mountain of debt. He can kick back and think, take long trips, or take care of his family; he has choices. He has both feet planted firmly on solid ground.

It is of course not the case that credit is totally unknown. The entrepreneurs in the city do take on credit from time to time. But they don't do so to excess. Remember that the existing monetary system is 100% reserve commodity money: money from thin air at artificially low interest rates does not exist. And the money that is available for credit — this must be said again — first has to be saved. Someone must have chosen to forgo consumption.

In addition, the entrepreneurs only take on credit when they are reasonably certain that they can meet all their loan obligations. They calculate their investments extremely carefully and they build up solid safety buffers for cases in which business is bad. The use of external capital (borrowed money) is also correspondingly low.

Because people rarely take on debt and because they usually consume less than they produce, the capital stock increases and both the people and the city get wealthier. And this increase in wealth benefits everyone, because purchasing power continually grows. At the same time, the taxes raised by the king are minimal. Usually, a family in the city only needs one income to take care of its needs and look after grandma, who lives with them. Women have choices too, and can thus focus on raising the children if they want to do so.

Uh, oh. Now we have opened a can of worms. This image goes completely against today's concept of the role of the genders. But don't get us wrong. Nothing would be further from the truth than us wanting women to focus on child-raising instead of working and fulfilling themselves in a career. Yet the question still remains, how many women work today because they really want to, rather than because their family needs that income to live ...

We are of the strong opinion that — after taking out taxes, social transfers, and permanent monetary devaluation — people have too little income left to be able to voluntarily decide for themselves whether one parent should focus on raising children or not. As a result, more and more small children and very young kids spend their days in state-supported day care centers. Only experts can know whether those day care centers are right for small children and what long-term effects reduced contact with the parents in the first few years have on them. But the fact remains that today, the option hardly exists to have one of the parents taking care of the kids during the day. And most women are — yes, we know, it is not politically correct to say this — biologically just better at that. They can breast-feed the baby and are generally better at calming babies and kids down than are men. But it doesn't matter, because continual price increases and high taxes take this choice away from parents.

But why are the taxes so high? Because someone has to pay to keep those day care centers open, right? Circular, isn't it? Parents are soaked financially to pay for day care services which, without that soaking, they might not need in the first place. And who does this help? Who gains power by doing this? You know this already …

Back to our small city. There, the parents can freely decide whether one parent will remain at home with the kids or whether both will have a career outside the home. They are not under the financial pressure that *both* of them have to work to provide their family with sufficient income. This is because the taxes in the city are extremely low. Of course, there are some families who don't have enough money and so both parents *have to* work. But that is an exception.

And when the parents want to work, they pay a nanny — out of their own pockets. Or maybe grandma takes care of the kids, if she lives with the family.

In any case, no one in the city is dependent on welfare payments from the king. (Nor does he provide any.) It is the people themselves who provide help and support to each other in times of trouble. You probably are now thinking that *the authors can't be serious. People supporting each other? That's totally unrealistic!* Well, today in our fast-paced world, in which everything is getting more expensive, the tax burden is becoming more and more intolerable, and insecurity with regard to wealth and property is huge, it is getting much harder for people to help each other. But hand on your heart. Have you never helped someone? Have you never tossed a coin into the hat of a street musician? Have you never given a friend advice, or helped a family member?

Whoever believes that family and friends won't help each other is the one living in a fantasy world.

In our city, the willingness to help is strong. The people in the city — thanks to the low taxes and lack of fast rising prices — also have the means to help and are not only materialistic. They hardly have to think about their savings and investments due to the stability of money. They also do not have to invest all their money in a way that earns the highest returns, for fear of the future and of their creditors. Non-commercial uses of income are thus very common. People do not live under a crushing mountain of debt that forces them to work. They have enough time to work *pro bono,* as volunteers, and to help others. Envy is almost unknown. And envy and the materialist striving for financial gains are *exactly* the factors that prevent people from supporting others in need. And as the king does not provide any welfare payments that could be used as an excuse not to help, the willingness to help is very high.

And now let us bring up a very important point. We have already discussed the fact that in our city, private people hardly have any debt and that only enterprises and business people use credit to finance themselves. The result is that the interest rates in our city are quite low. The lower the total interest that has to be paid in relation to the productive capacity of an economy, the lower the interest burden on the whole system.

And for exactly this reason, life in the city is not as hectic. Of course, people have to do their work; the city has not become a utopia of leisure. But they don't rush through their day. "More and more and faster and faster" is unknown. People have time for the nicer things in life. They often take time off, take care of their kids themselves, they have time to reflect, they can have cultural discussions, they can participate in sports, and they put a great emphasis on education and manners. And there is time for spiritual experiences too. In short, most people are relaxed, in balance, happy, and content.

But one day a man named *John Law* comes to town and pays the king a visit. (That this man has the same name as the man who caused one of the biggest paper money bubbles of all time in the 18th century, is just a coincidence.) Law's visit comes at a very good time for the king. Recently, some citizens have suggested that they could take care of their own security, at a higher quality than the king is currently providing, and cheaper than the king too. This new trend towards self-sufficiency and independence is threatening to the king's position. Who knows, the people might think to ask, "why do we need a sovereign at all?"

Of course, the king is not pleased, since he makes a good living off of his security services for the people. People might conclude that they do not want his services anymore, and then he would lose most of his income. What to do? The king needs to find a justification for his own position, maybe some set of new services only he can provide. He would need to convince the people that only he can perform these new tasks. Or, at least, that he could do it better than the citizens themselves. In this way, he would again make the citizens dependent upon him.

But how to do this? Most new services would cost a lot of money that the king doesn't have. Not to mention the costs of advertising and educating the public regarding their need for the new services. So he plans to set up a public radio station that will talk about the importance of the new tasks, and he plans to nationalize schools in order to win over his subjects in their earliest years.

But he somehow needs to pay for all of this. How? Raise taxes? Not now. The king does not dare risk a tax revolt.

Thank God for the new advisor who just arrived! John Law suggests to the king that he get together with the gold warehouses and grant them the legal right to issue warehouse receipts over and above the quantity of gold actually deposited. The additional issuance of warehouse receipts would increase the money supply. In addition, Law suggests that the king get rid of that "barbarous relic," gold, in the near future, and introduce a progressive modern paper currency. Paper being easier to increase, which brings with it big advantages.

If loans could be created out of thin air, people would not need to save as much and could fulfill their wishes immediately. Through increases in the money supply, the king could afford to undertake additional projects which would create jobs. The lowered interest rates would trigger an economic boom. And, the king could also take advantage of the credit himself. The king could then finance all kinds of benefits and welfare for the people. All of that would distract people — and, what is much more important for the king, it would make the people more dependent on him.

The king finds it hard to wrap his mind around all this, but he follows John Law's suggestion and pulls all gold coins out of circulation and exchanges them for freshly printed paper money notes. Trading in gold and owning gold is made illegal. The currency printing press works hard. The new paper currency circulates throughout the realm.

Because they only hold fractional reserves, the banks can create money out of thin air at favorable rates and lend it to businesses.

The result is predictable. It is like a dam breaking. The interest rates fall, and business owners start all kinds of new projects. During the boom, almost all the prices rise: wages, shares, real estate. Everyone is happy: workers, company managers and entrepreneurs, bankers, shareholders, and the king. And everyone begins to believe that people can get rich quickly, without having to work hard. During the artificially created boom which was unleashed by credit expansion and euphorically celebrated by the media, the people of our city — who had up until that time been so relaxed and calm — are becoming stressed out and tired.

Not being used to getting so much money without working, many people act irresponsibly. Short-term speculative operations and headline-making company takeovers are financed with the new money. An almost feverish party mood and great optimism ripples through the economy. People get the idea that it is possible to earn huge profits in a short amount of time, and they pursue those possibilities. The times change. Hard work, saving, and discipline are no longer necessary to get rich. Rather, stock market speculation or risky investments make (some) people rich overnight.

Later, the grisly end finally comes: the inevitable bursting of the speculative investment bubble, which was not financed by real savings but by the creation of new money. The economic collapse demoralizes an entire generation. Wealth disappears as fast as it had appeared. In their sudden poverty, many throw their moral principles overboard. The new booms and busts that recur in the city have devastating social effects. Incredible, isn't it? Did you think something like this could happen? These are the effects of a new monetary order!

The king finds the new economic cycles of benefit to himself. He and John Law celebrate behind closed doors.

This is because the new financial instability threatens the economic existence of many people and provides the impetus for additional regulations and government interventions. The king now has a new field of activity. He regulates the banks and the insurance companies, creates state welfare safety nets like state unemployment insurance, and bails out companies with a lot of employees that have gotten themselves into trouble.

But wholly aside from the devastating business cycles that now appear in our city, the state paper money is a cultural shock. Enterprises are relatively fast to act, but it takes a while for people to take the step of applying for a private loan. But because the prices of goods and services don't stop rising, and because the interest rates have fallen due to the additional money (created out of thin air), people start to have a change of heart. More and more, those who saved before buying now experience rising prices before they can save up the required capital. And those who act immediately and go into debt appear to be the winners. They are already living in their new homes and enjoying their credit-financed new goods — which continually rise in price — while the careful ones are still saving.

Our fisherman is among the careful ones who have not embraced the new cheap-money ways. He hoards his savings in cash, as his father, grandfather and great-grandfather did. Being the upright and law abiding citizen that he is, he gives up his gold and in return is given paper money. The king is now continually printing new money while the banking sector provides credit out of thin air. The effect of this constant supply of new money is that the prices no longer fall, the way they had in the past, but rise.

As the fisherman retires, he finds out that he is sitting on a mountain of paper money that is no longer sufficient to pay for his living expenses. A frightening realization for the fisherman and many of his generation!

The values upon which the previously successful city society was based are now questioned and shaken to their core. Saving, careful long-term thinking, and planning no longer bring the self-sufficiency they did before. Instead of being a proud and independent owner of his capital, which his father and grandfather were, the fisherman is now practically a have-not. It comes in handy that the king has introduced a state pension system. It functions on the principle of a pay-as-you-go scheme. The active working population sends "contributions" (taxes) to the king, who then sends them on to the retirees.

The children of the fisherman are quite happy about this system, as they do not have to support their poor father in his retirement. "Society" now does that. One of the fisherman's sons decides not to have children of his own. Why should he, when it is so stressful? After all, the costs of raising children are borne by the parents, but the "benefits" (the taxes collected from the children once they start working) are socialized and paid to all retirees, even those who are childless. Would it amaze you to learn that the birth rate in our city now falls sharply?

If you expected the new monetary order in the city to leave the social structures of the city untouched, you were wrong. Holding cash is becoming more and more unattractive. Corporate stock and other financial assets are no longer bought after careful saving, but on credit. The continual rise in prices devalues debts. Financial assets and real estate can be offered as collateral for loans in order to take on more debt and to buy more goods before the prices rise further. This makes financial assets much more attractive than they were at the time of the gold currency. Because of this, the prices of financial assets and real estate rise relative to the prices of other goods and services, and most importantly they rise faster than wages. Instead of saving for ten years to buy a home as his father did, the fisherman's son now has to wait 20 years before he can buy one.

Because it takes longer and longer to save enough, rising socially also becomes more difficult. Anyone who owns assets like company shares has an advantage, because the share prices are rising rapidly. And anyone who has assets can use them as collateral to obtain additional loans and buy even more real estate and shares, before the price rises even more and it becomes too expensive for middle-class people to buy. The new monetary order shatters the old concept of society. It is replaced by a class of asset-rich super-wealthy people on the one side, and a non-asset owning class of poor people on the other.

Is it any wonder that the paper money refashions society? Anyone who can, buys stuff on credit before prices rise. It is a brutal competitive battle. The faster you are, the better deals you get. Or to put it another way: the faster you go into debt, the better. The pressure is intense: you go into debt to obtain goods, and then you have to run like a hamster on a wheel to pay off that debt. This is in contrast with older times: The natural abhorrence against debt that people had in earlier days is disappearing fast. The seductive temptation of cheap money pulls many into a debt-driven lifestyle. People feel better when they are not alone in their circumstances — and now, almost everyone has debt.

And what about the business environment? Does it suffer, too? We have already seen how the ongoing economic cycles are demoralizing. Businessmen change how they run their companies in a fundamental way in a paper money economy. Company managers and entrepreneurs take on more risky investments. Money and credit appears to be available in abundance. Debts rise, and with it the entire debt burden, despite the continually falling interest rates.

But don't get the idea that interest rates are the problem, and that if they were reduced to zero, people would be free of their interest bondage, as some interest rate critics claim.

This is total nonsense. Interest rates arise out of our nature as human beings. Interest rates exist because of how we act. We prefer to reach our goals sooner rather than later. People prefer present goods, such as existing money, as opposed to future goods, for example money available in ten years. Anyone offering future goods (money in ten years) against highly valued present goods (money today) will have to accept a discount (for example 10,000 dollars in ten years for 8,000 dollars today). Interest is implied in the logic of human action, to put it in economic terms. The so-called time preference, i.e., the preference to consume sooner rather than later, manifests itself in the interest rate. If people are more long-term oriented, and thus willing to forgo present needs to have *more* in the future, then economists speak of a low time preference. But if people are consumption-oriented and thus are not willing to forgo things so easily, but would rather borrow money to make their purchases now, then they speak of a high time preference. The greater the time preference, the higher the rate of discount on future goods. Underlying this discount rate is the natural interest rate. And it cannot be eliminated in a world in which people live. A prohibition on interest would be fatal, because credit has an important allocation function in a market economy. Credit markets channel resources from savers to investors and workers, and this in turn allows for enormous increases in societal wealth over time.

Back to our city. Financing from equity capital (capital of one's own) and retained earnings is falling. *Credit* is the new "in" thing.

The fisherman's son quickly understands this. He was just able to prevent the family business from going under by discarding his father's thrifty values and taking on a loan at the same bank that gave him a mortgage to buy his house. The fisherman's son and his contemporaries are becoming dependent on banks and the financial industry, which now has its hands in everything. The financial sector is the true guiding force of the economy — thanks to the privilege of being able to create money out of thin air. This privilege generates its own power, as if by magic.

And company managers and entrepreneurs are drawn in by this magic power. Having fast access to the source of the new money becomes more important: having connections in the financial industry is essential for business success. Solidity, long-term thinking, and a skill in creating better products at lower prices recedes into the background.

Just as the new monetary system favors those who already have money, it also favors large, established enterprises at the expense of small ones, which can offer little by way of collateral for new loans. (And never mind the ones that do not even come into being due to the power of the established ones …) After all, people now need credit. Savings alone are no longer adequate to start a new company. The friends of the king are particularly close to the banking system. They have fast and easy access to the source of new money. They create new banks and industry conglomerates. They are very willing to take risks, because they can assume that if they run into trouble, they will be bailed out — with new money.

Short-term thinking focused on fast profits spreads. This is because the stability of continually falling prices no longer exists. And economic booms and busts follow one after another. This makes long-term planning harder. Insecurity rises. Instead of engaging in the creation of long-term value, managers now attempt to exploit the boom phases to make as much money as possible. Because who knows what will happen in five or ten years? In addition, asset prices continue to rise. And in order not to fall behind, many prioritize making a lot of money fast. Unscrupulous, selfish, short-term thinking managers are more and more common in the once peaceful city by the lake. Previously, managers identified with their company and its workers. Loyalty and a sense of close connection to the owners of the company — who in some instances were associated with the company for several generations — was more important to people than making fast money. Now, one debt-financed company takeover — also called *leveraged buyout* — follows another.

Sometimes the managers don't even know who the owner of their company is. Are you surprised that a long-term relationship with the company is becoming more and more rare? Their own private mountain of debt also makes managers more short-sighted and focused on material gain. They change employers more often — always in the search of a job that pays more. Business values like integrity, solidarity, and caring for the employees, as well as a broad perspective, are lost in favor of a short-term drive for profits. Whoever can get a mega-bonus goes for it, even if he has to do things that will hurt the company over the long term.

Oh, and the king? We almost forgot about him. How does the new money system affect him? The king also starts to go into debt. Based on Law's advice, he has come up with various social welfare programs for his citizens. He introduces insurance for cases in which someone is unemployed or injured. Mothers receive a child-raising allowance after the birth of a child. This is all paid for out of taxes — which are higher than they were before — and … with debt. Newly created money.

Every day, the king thinks up new ideas to help his subjects. He allows himself the luxury of setting up a committee of experts who all get a high salary from him. What they do to earn their money is to provide the king with ideas on what additional services he can introduce and how they should be organized. It is a dream for many intellectuals to be able to reorder the world to their liking! They think they know what is best for everyone. The paper money system provides them with the financial means to implement their schemes. Does it surprise anyone that journalists, commentators, teachers, and professors do not question the paper money system?

The king profits from the general instability and insecurity created by the new money system. Because entrepreneurs and business owners take on more and more debt, they increasingly get into financial trouble, particularly during times when interest rates rise. One of the first measures they then take is to lay workers off, especially in a recession. Unemployment poses a more difficult problem to those affected than it did before, when people had little or no debt. Due to the high levels of debt, people now have very little room for error, and even a short period of unemployment can put families in financial jeopardy. Many do not have financial reserves — people have gotten used to not saving. Financial problems are not good for family life. Particularly when people used to be able to afford anything they wanted — paid for on credit of course — and suddenly the exact opposite is true.

It is just as well that as of late the king has shown a willingness to care more for the needs of his subjects. They can count on him. He is always there for them, a true caring and providing leader. And the king intended this: he wanted to make people dependent on him and his social welfare programs. And his plan works. Instead of taking care of their own security and not relying on the king at all, as the people originally wanted, they now have different worries.

In the city, people think more and more short term. The social time preference rate rises. Less is saved. Economic growth, which was so impressive in the past, slows down. Hans-Hermann Hoppe, in his book *Democracy — The God That Failed*, describes the effects of today's common public social welfare programs:

> *"Every form of government welfare — the compulsory wealth or income transfer from 'haves' to 'have-nots' — lowers the value of a person's membership in an extended family household system as a social system of mutual cooperation and help and assistance. Marriage loses value. For parents the*

> *value and importance of a good upbringing (education) of their own children is reduced. Correspondingly, for children less value will be attached and less respect paid to their own parents." (pp. 182–83)*

This sounds terribly conservative, doesn't it? So perhaps it is time to set this book aside for a moment and reflect. A family also has practical constraints that derive from scarcity. The state cannot change that and abolish scarcity. The state merely uses the welfare benefits to give us the illusion that it can. And people let themselves be fooled. The state is not able to magically create resources. It can only spend what it has already extracted from civil society, whether through taxes or through money creation.

Why do so many marriages end in divorce? No one seems to want to go without or to do with less these days. Selfishness is spreading. People want more and more of everything. And they want it now. Family is increasingly not part of that picture. If having a lot of children was a good way to ensure one's old age in the past, today, that would mean the risk of poverty. And when parents have kids, then they send them to day care. In an interview with the Ludwig von Mises Institute of Germany, journalist Birgit Kelle, a mother of four, said, "*The state takes our money, our time, and — as of recently — also our children, and then it comes back to us with its more than 150 different family-oriented political (welfare) programs, through which they merely give back to us that which they previously took away from us.*"

A state paper money system is a true cultural shock for a society used to good money, like our good old city. Instead of waiting patiently, people are pressed into debt slavery. People drive prices up due to the goods they purchase with new loans they have taken on. Society becomes more materialistic. Taking on debt and investing money starts to take on a central role in people's lives. In earlier times, people saved gold coins in cash. Today, one has to go into debt and spend a lot of time investing money in order to stay afloat. There is less and less time for the nice things in life, culture, sports, and family. Because in a debt-driven economy, time is money. There used to be stability. Hard work, thrift and foresight paid off. Today, assets and acquisitions are unsafe — the motto is to make as much money as possible so as not to fall behind or go under. Otherwise you might become a kind of ward of the paternalistic state and get caught in its net. Does it surprise you that psychological illnesses in the population have increased in the recent past, in a population that is under more and more pressure?

Summary:

What occurred in our imaginary city in a short period of time, practically within a generation, has taken place in the real world over the past 100 years or so. And it is not over yet. The destruction of the gold standard and the turn to immaterial state money have permanently changed people's behavior. Inflationary paper money has created a debt economy. It has made people more and more dependent on the financial industry and the state — which both have expanded to an ominous degree. The slavery to high levels of debt together with the welfare state, also sponsored by paper money, have torn people loose from their roots. And to the extent to which people become dependent on the "provider-state," they are left less dependent on the help of those close to them, primarily the family. Social bonds break. The ethical mortar that holds society together falls apart. This is because the family communicates values and norms. The collapse of the family in the wake of bad money and the welfare state also promotes a serious moral crisis. In short: bad money makes people increasingly dependent, adolescent, socially isolated, torn from their roots, careless, unscrupulous, egotistical, materialistic, superficial, stressed, and depressed.

7. What happens when the state intervenes in everything

"The idea that there is a third system — between socialism and capitalism, as its supporters say — a system as far away from socialism as it is from capitalism but that retains the advantages and avoids the disadvantages of each — is pure nonsense."

- Ludwig von Mises

What do the monetary system, the health care system, the education system, and the energy sector have in common? Right. They are all run by the state, at least to a large extent. Most people don't even question why this is so. Let us now turn the discussion to why state intervention in the economy is bad. The ideal situation would be that the state does not intervene anywhere. Are you shocked that we would say such a thing? Notice the way politicians react to a new law that has gone into effect — they immediately begin proposing improvements to it. If political decisions and laws were well-thought-out and meaningful, they would not have to be modified right after being passed. By the way, "intervention" is really a misleading term — it really means that the state does not let the people pursue their own goals, but forces its own goals on them.

The state does intervene with physical violence or the threat of physical violence. Roland Baader in his book *Freiheitsfunken II* (*Sparks of*

Freedom), *Lichtschlag Medien, 2012, p. 62*) described the politicians' need to be constantly "doing something" in his unique style:

> *"The political class has to justify its reason for existing by doing something. But because it makes everything that it touches much worse, it is forced to make changes all the time; that means that it has to do something because it has already done something. It would not have to do anything if it had not already done something. If we only knew what to do to stop it from doing things."*

One cannot describe politics and politicians more accurately than that.

Our politicians act as if they can reshape the social and economic world to be just the way they want it. And because of their permanent need to act and their continual interference in the economy, they create the impression that they are actually capable of doing that. This is egomania. We want to destroy this mindset, this irrational belief, once and for all.

Thorsten Polleit hit the nail on the head in *Der Hauptstadtbrief* (*Letter from Berlin*), Issue 10/2013):

> *"What drives the supporters of interventionism is the opinion that through government interventions results can be achieved that are better than when the free market reigns. They are of the opinion that interventionism is a possible middle way between the capitalist (free market) system and socialism (collective ownership of the means of production). The interventionists thus believe that through interventionism, the 'good sides' of capitalism and socialism can be made use of while the bad sides can be excluded."*

To put it very simply, the belief is: *So we want some capitalism, because we are all a bit greedy and capitalism does in fact deliver the goods. But because we are also nice and socially minded people, not too much of it.* Seriously? Can that work? No! Unfortunately, being "a little pregnant" is not possible. And the politicians have created a successful business model for this: We will let the market economy first do something, but as soon as we don't get the outcome we desire, we call that "market failure" and government steps in.

To understand the results of interventionism, let's return to our now familiar city. We haven't been there for a while and should have a look ...

In the meantime, things have gone downhill in our city. About half of the dairy cows in the area have died from some disease. The result: milk is very scarce and the price has risen sharply. People complain about the high price of milk to the king, saying that he should intervene and do something. The king, of course, wants the people to like him, and he issues a proclamation: the price of a gallon of milk cannot exceed one-tenth of a gold dollar (which is what the currency is called now). By doing this he is setting a *maximum* price *below* the market price.

All his subjects are happy with this decree, except for the farmers. For many of them, milk production at the price set by the king is unprofitable. Although most farmers have lost about half of their herd of cows and half as many cows only eat half as much, the farmers' *fixed* costs have not been reduced by half. (That is why they are called "fixed" costs.) Some dairy farmers therefore decide to get out of the farming business. They slaughter most of their animals except what is needed for their own use, and only produce milk for their own consumption. The milk supply falls further. Only a few farmers who are very efficient in milk production remain in business. But of course the milk they produce is no longer sufficient to supply all the people. In order to reduce demand, the king's next proclamation will therefore be: *From now on, milk consumption will be limited to one pint per person per day.*

What happens next is protest marches toward the king's castle. The people are enraged and demand that their sovereign do something! And he acts by turning the screws of interventionism even tighter.

The king prohibits all further slaughter of cows, as well as the use of cows for the farmers' own consumption of milk or meat. Anyone who has a cow must by law use it for milk production, and must sell the entire production at the imposed maximum price or less. This move brings with it a short-term relief. More milk flows into the stores.

But for the farmers, the situation just became worse. They are practically forced into supplying milk at a loss. Their production costs in the form of wages, energy, agricultural equipment leases, and so on, exceed the permitted legal sales price for the milk. The result: cows that die of illness or old age are not replaced. Cow breeders get out of the business. It is even rumored that individual farmers are poisoning their own animals to avoid further losses.

Milk production falls even further. This is the opposite of what the king wanted to achieve with his interventions! But he does not give up. Next, he regulates the input prices of the farmers and sets an upper limit for what they have to pay for agricultural wages, equipment leases, and energy.

With their costs reduced by decree, it is again profitable for the farmers to produce milk. The shelves fill up again. The king is satisfied with his interventionist measures, believing that they have taken care of the problems — and then he hears the latest news. The farmers can't get anyone to work for them anymore. Agricultural workers are leaving in droves to find work elsewhere — in sectors where the wages have not been artificially lowered. Agricultural equipment is no longer being produced. Fields are left fallow. The king gets mad and decides to act again. He regulates the wages in other sectors, as well as the input prices of the equipment manufacturing industry, and orders that the fields be planted. Slowly but surely, it has gotten to the point where the king sets *all* the prices. The spiral of interventions has come to the last thread of the screw. Welcome to socialism!

Of course, from the very beginning, the king could have intervened in milk production and could have let the bureaucrats determine the production, distribution, and prices of milk. Or put more simply: he could have nationalized milk production from the outset — with the same result.

Anyone who has lived in communist East Germany, Cuba, or the Soviet Union can tell you how well the supply of consumer goods works under communism. If you want to experience socialism yourself, go spend your next vacation in North Korea. There, you can see how socialism really works — or more precisely, how it does *not* work.

But why doesn't socialism work? The answer is simple: In a socialist system, there is no private property. The state owns all property. Or "the people" own it, as these states like to claim, because it sounds better. The production of goods is not determined by consumer demand. State bureaucrats determine what should be produced. They decide what goods should be manufactured and in what quantities, and who will receive them.

Ludwig von Mises, in his book *Socialism: An Economic and Sociological Analysis* from 1922 demonstrated that *socialism cannot work.* He proved that economic calculation is impossible under socialism. Basic bookkeeping and accounting allow a business owner to know if he has made profits or losses. This is enormously important in a market economy.

Profits show that the factors of production have been combined in a way that increases value: the selling price of the product is above the expenses required to obtain the resources needed to manufacture it. On the other hand, losses show that resources were wasted: we would have been better off if they had been used to produce something else.

In socialism there is public or common ownership of the factors of production: raw materials, machines, and factories are all owned by the state. For this reason, there are no exchanges of goods and services and thus no market prices for raw materials, machines, and factories. And without market prices, economic calculation cannot take place. So people don't know if they have made a profit or a loss. They cannot even calculate the cheapest way to manufacture something. Should the conductor used in computer chips be of iron, steel, copper, silver, gold, or silicon? The chip would be just as fast. But the socialist planner is in the dark: without a market price, the decision will be arbitrary and based on the planner's whim.

Back to our city. Let's rewind and go back in time to the moment when the people complain to the king about the high milk prices. This time, the king responds differently. He calls in a consultant, one who understands economics. He has some uncomfortable suggestions for his new client: he advises the king NOT to intervene and NOT to set a maximum price for milk. The king at first is skeptical and asks himself: *What do I need a consultant for, if all he can tell me is to do nothing?* But the consultant explains his ideas to the king in detail, and he is convincing. And the king does … *nothing.*

The king doesn't need to do anything, because the price of milk rises fast as a result of the deaths of the sick cows — and that is normal. After all, the high price of milk tells the market participants that milk is very scarce relative to demand at the moment. The profits of the dairy farmers rise. For those prone to envy, that might be very painful at first.

"We have to buy your expensive milk and you are filling your pockets with cash," many will say. But will this condition last? Of course not. What will happen?

Some of the dairy farmers will earn more money and they buy additional dairy cows. Other farmers, who were not engaged in milk production at all, have noticed the higher milk prices and see an opportunity to make money in that field, and so they also get into milk production. Cattle breeders are flooded with orders and they develop more efficient ways to breed cows.

Cows that were destined to be slaughtered are now put into milk production instead. The current technique used for production of milk is not adequate to handle the increased quantity of milk needed; it takes too long and some of the milk spoils before it can get to the market. An inventive person, who sees the possibility of making some money, creates a pump that speeds up milk production and reduces waste during the process.

Consumers also have to take into account the higher price of milk. They reduce their milk consumption and look for milk substitutes.

The next door neighbor's kitten no longer gets dairy milk that is now too expensive, but water or goat's milk.

You can imagine how this story ends. After more dairy cows fill the milking stalls on the farms and additional milk producers enter the market, the quantity of milk rises. At the same time, consumers have become thriftier and are using substitutes for milk where possible. So supply is up, and demand is down. As a result, the price of milk falls.

As we have seen, people in a free market solved the problem all by themselves, with entrepreneurial foresight and creativity. Fully without coercion, without police, military, judges, or prisons. No state intervention was required. In contrast, the original interventions by the king were counterproductive, as we saw.

In a competitive free market, enterprises compete in guiding capital and resources to where they are most urgently needed. If the entrepreneurs are right, they earn profits. If they are wrong, they suffer losses. If they are really right, they earn high profits. If very wrong, immense losses. Losses are a sign that capital and resources have been wasted. And this not only makes the entrepreneur poorer, but also society, and we all suffer.

Isn't it strange that entrepreneurs are not criticized by politicians and media commentators for the losses they incur, but for profits that are "too high." From the consumers' point of view, the opposite should be the case. The higher the profit, the better. Higher profits mean that scarce resources have been used to meet the needs of people. And that is what we care about, right? In the market economy, the entrepreneur or business owner is merely the man at the helm, the taker of orders. The man at the helm tries to estimate the future commands of the "captain." And the "captain" is the consumer. The "captain" — and we are all the "captain" — determines what things will be produced, and how they are manufactured, by simply making choices in the marketplace to purchase certain goods, and to pass other goods by.

An uncountable number of economically relevant decisions are made by millions of people every day in the country you live in. This is the *market*, which draws criticism from all sides. And politicians want to control this market with interventions. This is the *fatal conceit*, as Friedrich August von Hayek once called it. *We* refer to it as megalomania.

If a government or an agency of the state intervenes in the market, an existing problem will perhaps be solved — for the moment. But another will be created by the intervention, as we saw in the milk problem. Due to the price ceiling, some producers dropped out of the market and the supply of milk shrank. The king certainly did not intend for that to happen! Thus, each intervention must bring with it the next one, until in the end, everything is regulated. The market economy is thus increasingly burdened and robbed of its power.

What led to the downfall of the Roman Empire? In school, you were probably told that an increasingly decadent Rome was overrun by barbarian tribes. But that was not the real reason for the fall of Rome, as Ludwig von Mises shows in his book *Human Action.* Interventionism led to Rome's downfall. Or more precisely, the welfare state, which caused a spiral of interventions. Bad money also played an important role.

What? You have never heard this? But it is true. The barbarians had been pressing against the boundaries of Rome for centuries. A powerful, prospering Roman Empire found it easy to push them back — until the heavy burdens of the welfare state destroyed Roman society. The barbarians were then able to invade and occupy the weakened ruins of the former strong empire.

The downfall began when emperors found they needed to gain favor with the people through the strategy of *panem et circenses* — bread and circuses. Further attempts to gain favor with the masses was to nationalize the grain trade, the so-called *annona.* The emperor distributed grain at highly subsidized prices, or even at times for free. More and more people, the so-called *proles* (from which we have the term proletariat) lived off the largesse of the state. They became dependent on the *annona.* Today we say that they lived on welfare. To keep the masses quiet, gladiatorial fights were put on. In short, the emperors created a welfare state with its unavoidable and ever-rising costs.

But how to defray those costs? Without raising fees and taxes so high as to provoke revolts? The emperors had a very clever idea. You probably already guessed it: They manipulated the monetary system. More precisely, they reduced the quality of the coins, by smelting down old coins made of precious metals and reminting them after adding cheaper base metals like copper. They were thus able to expand the available number of coins, and in this way they were able to pay their expenses. A redistribution in favor of the state occurred, with the state as the first user of the new inferior money, at the expense of later recipients.

As a result of this inflationary policy, prices rose. The proletariat became restive. The emperors then decreed maximum prices. The price ceilings led many farmers to conclude that producing food was no longer profitable.

Farmers throughout Italy, who had up to that time produced food for the market and for the population of Rome, withdrew from exchange. Some limited themselves to production for their own use. Others moved from the farm to the city. Why produce grain at a loss when food was practically free in Rome?

The proletariat and the city of Rome expanded fast. And with it the costs of the welfare state. The division of labor which had been so well developed up until then, the intense exchange between the agrarian population and the cities across the entire Mediterranean, collapsed. Instead of productive specialization and exchange, inefficient autonomous production now reigned.

The welfare state, inflation, and interventionism dealt a death blow to the market economy. Rome was no longer able to pay for its legions of soldiers. The barbarians invaded and occupied the remains of the once flourishing empire, which finally fell in the 5th century A.D. Instead of a highly specialized division of labor and a market economy, there was now feudalism. A long and painful economic decline set in.

It is not a law of nature that civilization always advances and the living standard always improves. Far from it! Without the right legal, economic, and social conditions, such as private property, individual freedom and sound money, things can reverse and go downhill.

Peter Temin in his book *The Roman Market Economy* estimated that the average per-capita income fell greatly with the fall of the Roman Empire, permanently or at least for a long time. According to Temin, the standard of living enjoyed by the ancient Romans was only experienced again at the start of the modern era, around the year 1700. They were in a recession for a thousand years!

For a thousand years people were poorer than the Romans had been in the ancient era, thanks to the welfare state, financed by inflation, and interventionism.

Put down the book for a moment and think. Where would we be today if this thousand-year break had not occurred? What if people in classical times had just continued with their capital accumulation, division of labor and their economic and technical advances? It took 200 years from the start of the Industrial Revolution in the 18th century to the first moon landing. Just consider it with an open mind. Without the more than a thousand lost years, caused by interventionism and inflation, we might have been on the moon in the year 700 A.D. Or maybe in the year 1000. And where would that put us today? That is of course science fiction. We can only imagine what it would have been like.

We would also have to imagine a world with good money. We have no solid comparison with our current situation. We can only guess how robust, dynamic, and wealthy our current civilization would be today if governments had not destroyed the gold standard and replaced it with a paper money system that allows them to finance bloated welfare states.

We can only imagine how vibrant our civilization would be without today's tangle of regulations and taxes.

The people of communist East Germany had a comparison. They just had to look over the Berlin Wall to see the West's wealth of goods. They saw, were shocked and were appalled. They protested against their system. The Berlin Wall fell.

Today no one is protesting, because today we have no parallel society that we can look to that would show us how good things could be without paper money, welfare states, and bad governments. There is simply no way to know.

Our impoverishment today is not yet complete. Living standards are not falling. We are only poor compared to a world with sound money and without state intervention. If we could actually see this hypothetical world, as was the case for the people of communist East Germany, then people would be at the barricades; they would rise up and storm the central banks and the parliaments.

Even if our standard of living is not falling in absolute terms, the parallels between our economic situation today and the fall of the Roman Empire are striking and worrisome. Bread and circuses (for example election campaigns) are today incredibly expensive, and can barely be financed. Bad money and inflation are slowly destroying our standard of living. And interventionism is expanding at a rapid pace. There is hardly any area of life in which the state and government do not intervene. People are prevented from acting the way they would want to by interventions, regulations, laws and prohibitions. For example, an entrepreneur will abstain from an investment that would have created jobs if the project is no longer seen as profitable because of an increase in the legal minimum wage. Those jobs are *not* created. But no one talks about those uncreated jobs, because they have not been created, and are not visible.

Another important topic in the discussion of intervention in the market is the minimum wage, which was just introduced in Germany and has existed in the U.S. since 1938. The examples above have shown how different state interventions affect one another in such a way that the average person does not see the relationships, much less understand them.

Please recall Chapters 3 and 5. There we described in detail how the expansion of the money supply has a tendency to lead to income and wealth being redistributed from the bottom to the top income classes.

The expansion of the money supply and the manipulation of the interest rate downward are nothing but *interference* with money, nothing other than *intervention.* (Note that the nationalization of the monetary system is itself an intervention.) This intervention makes some poorer and some richer. As a tendency, price increases result in the lower and middle classes becoming poorer, and the rich — with their direct and faster access to the new money — become richer.

Over time, the lower income classes are able to buy less and less, because the purchasing power of their income falls due to inflation.

It is at this point that politicians, union leaders, and other well-meaning people take to the stage and speak for those whose wages are no longer sufficient to pay for their living expenses, and demand that a minimum wage be set by the state. Look at how these people speak into the microphones and how they always claim to know *exactly* what needs to be done: *We have to …*

"Have to" seems so harmless. But "have to" means that state coercion, physical violence, or the threat of force is needed to solve the problem. "Have to" means — ultimately — police and prison for those who do not obey. Why not just try voluntary agreement and contractual cooperation? Why always resort to coercion and force?

Can it really be that not one of these self-proclaimed experts knows that the inflation they are complaining about has been caused by government interventions in the first place? We ask in all honesty: *Is this possible*? It has to make one distrustful when topics such as money creation out of thin air and artificially low interest rates are totally ignored in *all* the discussions about the causes of our problems. In any case, all the "experts" are in agreement: *We have to do something! The state has to see to it that people can once again make a living from their labor.*

Initial government interventions in the form of *monetary expansion* and *low interest rate policies* are inevitably followed by the next market intervention: a *minimum wage law*. But this intervention also has consequences that no one wants: specifically, unemployment. You doubt that? Note, if the minimum wage is higher than the market wage, the demand for workers will *automatically* fall. Economically, a minimum wage is also called a minimum price: the opposite of a maximum price, as was the case with milk in our city. It represents a lower price limit. If farmers are guaranteed a minimum price of two gold dollars per gallon from the state, then the result will be huge unsellable surpluses — oceans of excess milk. Farmers produce like crazy and at the same time, the demand for milk falls. The same happens with a minimum wage. More and more people try to enter the labor market or to work longer hours, whereas they could have focused on their children or cultural pursuits, education, and other leisure activities. At the same time, demand for labor from potential employers falls. The result: legions of unemployed people.

And if a minimum wage of $10 per hour is good, why not $100 or $1,000? What would happen if a minimum wage of $10,000 per hour were set? Correct! Mass unemployment.

But normally minimum wages are much more moderate. And because only those people are excluded from the labor market whose productivity is under the minimum wage, it only affects a few. But these are exactly those people — people without a lot of qualifications and with a lower income — who were intended to be helped by those advocating a minimum wage.

If the legal minimum wage is followed by unemployment, you will not have to wait long before politicians focus on the next intervention: education and skills training for the unemployed, which will have to be paid for somehow. Politicians will now go to the media with the message: *Equality of opportunity must be achieved! We have to start with pre-school education. We need more public kindergartens and day care centers. So many parents can no longer afford to educate their children* (nor be trusted to do so), *because their level of education is low* (that is not spoken out loud, however*), and some because they just can't do it for lack of time.* Family life is increasingly brought under state influence. We already dealt with this topic in detail in the previous chapter.

Yet another intervention is the government promoted "energy switch" (the switch away from nuclear power to "green" energy) imposed in Germany and elsewhere; it is an example par excellence of state interventionism. You can directly observe the results of state intervention in the energy supply sector on your energy bill if you live in Germany. It has nothing to do with a market economy anymore. Perhaps *you* can still afford to subsidize this government nonsense with your own income, if you are rich enough. The single widow living alone and people living on low incomes certainly cannot do so.

In neighboring Austria, they are rolling on the floor laughing at the Germans. Especially when the sun is shining and there is constant wind in Germany and the momentary market price of energy is very low. Then the Austrians buy German energy — which was generated at a high cost — for a song, and use it to pump water into their mountain reservoirs. Later they use the stored water to generate cheap hydroelectric power, which they can sell back to Germany at a higher price!

One intervention follows another. Attempts are made to soften the effects of one state intervention by using further state interventions. One effect is, for example, that a single widow in Wanne-Eickel (a provincial German city) can no longer pay her energy costs, because the energy price she pays also has to pay for thc huge solar wind-farm in far-off Bavaria. But thank God there is the "energy-savings check" sent to her from Caritas, a charity, and from energy agencies and climate change agencies. Grandma is very happy about that, because otherwise she might have to sit in the dark. The catch is that the process is subsidized by the German Federal Environmental Ministry.

The Internet site of an energy-saving initiative in Germany states what would otherwise happen to many people in Germany without this assistance: *"The energy-saving check is an assistance that helps people help themselves and is intended to prevent low-income people from being left in the dark without electricity. Upon request, authorized households are visited by the energy-saving helpers, who will first determine energy and water consumption. Then free energy-saving devices specific to each household will be installed, and tips will be given on how to use them and how to be energy-efficient ... The energy-saving helpers will install free energy-saving lamps, water tap installations, humidifiers, TV switches and switchable power strips."* This sounds like Christmas!

Please don't misunderstand us. We are not criticizing the "energy-saving helpers." They no doubt do a lot of good. And also we don't intend to accuse the Bavarian large-scale farmers with their huge photovoltaic installations of being bad. They all act rationally. But state subsidies are flowing there. *Your* money is being spent there if you live in Germany. Money that the state takes from you *coercively*. Money that you could have used for your own purposes. Over time, all that adds up. You could have used that money to buy your wife a nice gift, or to save money for your children's education.

One way or another, state interventions lead to capital and resources not being used where they are needed most. For that to happen it is necessary that the free market, which discovers where these resources are most urgently demanded, is not distorted by interventions.

When someone writes and speaks as we do, you have to watch out that you are not pilloried because "higher" goals are considered more important, "higher" goals as defined by our all-knowing politicians along with others who represent labor unions and special interest groups.

Ludwig von Mises saw it that way. In 1944, in his book *Bureaucracy,* he wrote:

> *"But ours is an age of a general attack on the profit motive. Public opinion condemns it as highly immoral and extremely detrimental to the commonweal. Political parties and governments are anxious to remove it and to put in its place what they call the 'service' point of view and what is in fact bureaucratic management."*

Through ever greater state interventions in economic life, the profit motive of market participants is permanently distorted. People act differently than they would without state interference. In the end, everything is like a thick tangled web — overgrown and suffocating. So interwoven that the individual threads, or initial interventions, are no longer recognizable. The average person is no longer able to discern what has happened and the so-called experts are clueless. The state can do what they wish. The free market is buried under an interventionist avalanche.

The experts, by the way, are mostly economists. In actuality, universities breed "experts" who have studied macroeconomics and who favor intervention. Those students have learned that uncontrolled markets are unpredictable and do not function in an orderly fashion, and why the state needs to intervene to help them out.

Those "experts" find employment at government agencies and enterprises that then have to deal with the regulations. For example, students who specialize in monetary theory have good chances of getting a job at the central bank. Indeed, they will have learned that a paper money system is advantageous, and how to "fine-tune" the economy using the money supply and interest rate policy. And to reiterate: without state money and other interventions by the state, these economists would not be needed in the first place! It is thus not a surprise that most economists are in favor of state intervention, and that they accept the central bank and state money as if these institutions were ordained by God. Their jobs depend on it! If I eat the king's bread, I sing the king's song, as the saying goes. (There are apparently exceptions, as you have probably already noticed).

But back to the avalanche of interventionism. The interference of the state in the monetary system is just the beginning. Soviet politician and revolutionary leader Vladimir Lenin (1870–1924) was once reported to have said: The best way to destroy the capitalist system is to destroy the currency.

Lenin would have loved our current economic situation. René Scheu, the publisher of the libertarian-oriented magazine *Schweizer Monat* (*The Swiss Monthly*) has described our current environment as "semi-socialism." If a way is not found back to a free market economy and we continue down the path of more state interference and management, the road will end with total socialism.

We have already seen how our king could not stop once he began controlling the price of milk. The alternative would have been to give up all price controls and to allow the market to solve the problem.

When he did not do that, logically he had to take further steps. In the end, the king needed to monitor that the farmers did not evade his price controls. The people will perhaps attempt to obtain the much needed milk by paying higher prices. A black market will result. And how will the king prevent a black market? He will threaten people with steep penalties, and enforce them when perpetrators are caught. Maybe he will spy on his own people to uncover black marketeers of milk and prosecute them. Does that sound familiar? The East German communist state had such a system until 1989.

Of course, the blame would be put on others, for example those farmers who turn to the black market. The black market in East Germany was the solution to the problem of scarcity and a way to evade the impoverishing regulations. A black market is not a problem, but rather the market solution to the problems created by government! Without functioning black markets in Eastern Europe, socialism and communism would have collapsed much sooner.

Now please transfer this idea to the current financial crisis. Who do our politicians blame for these crises? Exactly. The "greedy speculators" and the bankers. In a 2008 interview in the German magazine *Stern*, German President Horst Köhler said that *the financial markets have turned into a monster.* This statement is even more notable considering that Köhler was the managing director of the International Monetary Fund (IMF) in 2004, before his election as German president in 2004. He should thus know the real causes of the crisis — the paper money, the central banks, and the fractional reserve banking system. But the blame is put on others. In doing so, it is easy to justify additional rules and regulations and to draw attention away from failed policies. The failures may be turned into an opportunity to introduce new taxes, for example a financial transaction tax: As they put it, *one must make those who caused the crisis participate in its costs.* Politicians make calculated use of envy and direct people's anger and rage in a focused way at entrepreneurs and the rich.

Consider for a moment in how many areas free price formation is not allowed today. Interest rates are manipulated by the central banks, a minimum level is set for wages, and the energy prices are driven up due to the state-ordered "energy switch" to green energy (in Germany). Another important area is the healthcare system, which is saturated by state regimentation and price setting. In Germany, all the insurance providers are forced to bill the same monthly fee, which eliminates competition. In the U.S., with Obamacare the government is beginning a takeover of the medical insurance.

Although the individual national governments in Europe are the true villains in this tale, the bureaucrats of the European Union are eagerly joining the party, overruling national bureaucrats and imposing additional regulations and guidelines over all the citizens of Europe. The ban on traditional lightbulbs is just the most trivial example! More and more, palpable pressure is put on the critics of increasing state influence. Most of all, critics of the EU are defamed and depicted as "anti-European." Yet it was competition and freedom that made Europe great, and not centralism and state *dirigisme* (strong state control of investments). The real Europeans are those who fight the EU Moloch. The "anti-Europeans" sit in Brussels, at the EU headquarters.

Summary:

State interference in economic life not only distorts the free interplay between market participants, it also leads to more and more interventions and thus to a ballooning of state power. Either earlier interventions must be cancelled, or new problems that were created have to be corrected with further meddling. An interventionist spiral is set in motion which further limits people's freedom. At the end of this path stands full totalitarian socialism. But ultimately socialism cannot work, because there is no price formation and thus no economic calculation is possible. Under socialism, capital and resources are wasted. Society becomes poorer. Maintaining a socialist system is only possible through more and more state surveillance and coercion.

The most pernicious of all interventions is the nationalization of money and with it the monopolization of money creation. This intervention is the trigger for numerous other interventions. The fall of the Roman Empire shows where the manipulation of money — coupled with an interventionist spiral — leads.

8. How it will all end

"What the people already ate, they will miss for decades when they are hungry."

- Roland Baader

As you can no doubt see, we are in big trouble. We won't get out of it without some painful steps. The cancer of state money has already spread throughout the body of the economy, doing extensive damage. For some time now, we have been living in a period of increasing impoverishment in relation to where we could have been without the interference of the state in our lives and the economy. The majority of people are clueless. But thanks to this book you are no longer one of them. You have been awakened from your fog of ignorance! Sometimes it is easier to live in ignorance. But it is too late for that now. And look on the positive side: you now know what is happening and can react appropriately.

The paper money system has done great damage to society. It has enabled the financing of huge "unfair states" and contributed to the decline of traditional institutions such as the family. Society has become much more materialistic. People plan short term and take on debt. The "de-socialization" caused by ever more burdensome governments pumped up on the drug of paper money is becoming increasingly worrisome. In the end, our individual liberty is overrun by the monetary printing press. The social redistribution results of the paper money system make states, banks, large enterprises, and the super-rich richer, but the poor and middle class poorer. A monetary divide is increasingly evident in society. Social conflicts are increasing and the real economy is buckling under the burden of the financial industry cartel.

One thing has to be made clear: misallocation caused by money production has already done enormous damage to real wealth. We just don't see it yet! Unfortunately we do not have a society to compare it to in which this waste did *not* occur.

State expenditures for welfare programs at home and military interventions abroad have caused increasing state debt and increasing budget deficits in the western world. This debt will never be able to be repaid, in real terms. The welfare state is, by the way, the greatest malinvestment of them all. It does not satisfy the needs of people cooperating freely among one another and would end quickly if it were not permanently subsidized by the money monopoly and tax money collected by coercion.

The cycles of artificial booms and recessions caused by the privileged banking system bring immense suffering to people. The financial crisis of 2008–2009 revealed the enormous amount of resources that disappeared into the chasm of the money system. Forever.

Was it really so bad, you think? Certainly you are overstating what happened!

The 2008 bailout orgy was without historical precedent. Banks, businesses, and even governments were rescued. Without pain, right? But have you noticed something strange? Did you lose your job or your savings? Were your taxes brutally increased in the past few years? Did your tax burden double? Probably not. How is the ongoing bailout financed? You already know: by new debt, by new money. This is what is so insidious about the state money system: it makes it possible to hide the true costs and losses which the system itself creates. It lulls people into a false sense of security. This false sense of security has been taken away from you. We warned you in the introduction to this book that unpleasant realities awaited you.

The big collapse did not happen in 2008. After the collapse of Lehman Brothers and the subsequent financial crisis, only part of the malinvestments were liquidated. Enterprises such as the troubled auto manufacturers and mortgage banks were rescued by the state; either by direct capital injections or indirectly through subsidies and state orders for goods and services. Bad private investments were turned into bad public debt — the process silent and lubricated with new money. This is because the state debt was financed indirectly with new money production. Central banks created new money with which the (commercial) banks and other economic "agents" then bought government bonds.

But it was not just the real economy that got into trouble. The bursting of the real estate bubble caused extreme losses for the banks. But these losses were also only partly recognized, and banks were saved all over the world by their respective national governments. As a result, the bad debt was transferred from the banks to their governments, but this does not mean that these debts have disappeared. Or do you believe that a hot potato just disappears when it is handed off? Someone has it. Ultimately it is all of us who have it, as will become obvious sooner or later. In the meantime, additional bad state debt has been added: for example through the increase in "social expenditures" in the form of support for the unemployed and through numerous economic programs meant to jump-start the economy. State debt since 2008 has exploded — and hovers over us like the Sword of Damocles.

In other words: The losses stemming from malinvestments were to a large part just shifted to the nation-states and to the balance sheets of the central banks. Neither the original investors nor the bank shareholders nor the bank creditors nor the holders of government bonds have yet written off the losses. The bad debt just keeps piling up in the form of national debt. But shifting around bad debts does not bring back lost wealth. The debts remain. When and how do you think the debt will catch up to us?

To pursue this question, let's return one last time to our imaginary city. For the sake of simplicity, let's assume that there are only two generations. The first is represented by the fisherman. He has been working hard for decades and saves for his retirement. He uses his old boat for his work. As dilapidated as it is, he will mothball it as soon as he goes into retirement. The fisherman invests his savings in bonds which are issued by a young captain, who represents the younger generation in our story. The young captain invests the fisherman's money (from the bonds) in a project that has a lot of promise. He starts building a new modern fishing boat. The captain wants the vessel to be larger and more efficient than the fisherman's dilapidated old boat. The captain will be able to catch enough fish to feed both of them with the new boat, when the fisherman is retired. The captain will then easily be able to repay the loan and the fisherman can enjoy his retirement.

Once the fisherman retires, he wants to use his savings. He wants to sell his bonds over time to buy the goods (fish) produced by the captain. But his plan will not work if the captain wasted his capital on malinvestments. If the capital was wasted, the bonds represent bad debt. The captain will find it impossible to repay the real value of the debt. He is not able to catch enough fish to feed both himself and the retired fisherman.

Why the captain cannot pay is ultimately not important. Maybe he is a con man and didn't even build the boat, but just used the fisherman's savings for his own consumption. Just as today the state gives tax money to welfare recipients who then just consume the funds. Or as today, with the state not investing contributions to the public pension system, but rather putting them into a pay-as-you-go system and funneling it to retirees — who then for the most part consume it.

The state pension system (Social Security in the U.S.) is dangerous because it simulates a replacement for savings. I don't have to save, I pay my retirement contributions, is what many think. But nothing is saved, it is simply transferred to others and to a large extent consumed. The pensions of the retirees (returns on their savings) are instead paid out of the contributions of wage earners — those currently working. This acts like a gigantic chain letter system, or pyramid scheme — just like the scam perpetrated by financial criminal Bernie Madoff. Madoff enticed many investors with enormous returns. And he used the money of the most recent investors to pay the older ones high returns, right up until the moment when his fraud was exposed. And it ended the way every pyramid scheme ends — with great losses suffered by most of the victims.

But the fisherman's money can be wasted in other ways. The captain can be highly decent and honorable, but the projects financed with the fisherman's capital could still fail — think of the malinvestments of the financial crisis in the real estate sector, for example.

Let's imagine that the boat was poorly built and sunk (malinvestment such as the real estate bubble) or that the captain never even built the boat, because he preferred to throw parties (malinvestment such as the welfare state). The assets that the fisherman thinks he owns are no longer there. The fisherman lived the entire time under the illusion that he was rich. He still owns those bonds, after all!

Now let's imagine that the king has introduced paper money and a central bank. To rescue the situation, the king buys out the captain's failed business (along with the sunken boat). This prevents a bankruptcy, which would have revealed the losses. Just as enterprises were bailed out by the government during the recent financial crisis!

The king could also choose to bail out the captain not by buying the business, but by making additional funds available, so that the captain can continue to operate his failing business. The king obtains the money by taking on debt himself — in other words issuing debt (bonds) and having the central bank buy up the bonds (just as central banks today buy up government debt). The king is not dumb, after all.

The captain could then pay the fisherman with freshly printed money, due to the intervention of the king. As an alternative, the central bank could print money and directly buy up the fisherman's bonds. Thus the bad investments (in the form of bonds) end up on the central bank's balance sheets, or in the king's coffers.

The fisherman could thus continue to live under the illusion that he is rich because he owns state debt, paper money, or bonds of a nationalized or state-subsidized firm. The fisherman's situation is comparable to ours today: many people feel rich and secure, because — on paper — they have assets saved, because they own government bonds, bank deposits, or bond funds. Or because they have a life insurance policy or retirement insurance (banks, mutual funds, and life insurance companies are heavily invested in government debt).

At any rate, the wealth destruction (the sinking of the boat, or money wasted on a partying lifestyle), in other words, the malinvestment, cannot be undone.

In the end, the fisherman will not be able to eat the bonds, the paper money, or the financial claims that he owns. There is simply nothing there to back them up. In our example, given the lack of a boat no one is catching fish today in our imaginary city, so the available fish will not be sufficient to feed both the fisherman (the older generation) and the captain (the younger generation). And what will the fisherman do then?

It is the same for people today. Many believe that they have wealth that in reality does not exist. The assets were squandered directly or indirectly through malinvestments made by governments. Governments squandered the money in state welfare projects and on promises they cannot keep through the state pension systems; they bailed out unhealthy and failing companies by creating artificial markets, they granted subsidies and capital injections. Government debts exploded.

Many people believe that paper assets that they own in the form of government bonds (debt), mutual funds, insurance policies, bank accounts, and other claims will assure them of a comfortable retirement. But in retirement, they will only be able to consume that which they have saved in the form of real goods, and — more importantly — what is produced in the real economy. But the actual productive capacity of the economy is seriously damaged and diminished due to government intervention. Today's paper assets are covered by a lot of hot air. The continual shifting of bad debt to governments and central banks cannot undo the destruction of wealth. The day of reckoning will come sooner or later. Savers and retirees will notice at some point that the real value of their assets is lower than they had thought it would be. How this day of reckoning comes is up in the air. We can only hope that growth through technological innovation, capital accumulation, and an increasing division of labor at home and in other parts of the world will help to soften the eventual blow.

That we have arrived at this point cannot now be changed. But was the situation really unavoidable? Did it have to be this way? If you have read this far, you will know the answer: once we bet on the wrong horse, the catastrophe became unavoidable.

The reason can be found in the system itself. The pure paper money system that we have lived under for over 40 years encourages the taking on of too much debt, and carries with it the seeds of its own destruction.

In a coercive fiat monetary system, money can be created out of thin air on a computer. The temptation to take advantage of this power is almost irresistible.

In a paper money system, the money supply and prices have a tendency to continually rise. Saving cash to acquire assets is not advisable in such a system. It is much smarter to go into debt to acquire assets such as real estate and to pay back the debt later with money that by then will be worth less, or even worthless.

Those economic agents who hope to be bailed out through the production of new money have a particularly strong incentive to take on a large amount of debt. Large organizations, primarily banks, and governments can hope to be too big to fail.

As if that were not enough, the fractional banking system causes more and more booms and busts. There is no complete liquidation in the bust phase. On the contrary, new money is produced in order to slow down the adjustment process or to prevent it completely. The imbalances slowly accumulate. And then we start from a place of ever higher levels of bad debt, and embark on a new cycle.

The same system has been in place for the past 40 years. During crises, the interest rates are lowered and over-indebted economic actors are bailed out with new money.

A paper money system thus resembles a snowball that is let go on the top of a mountain and rolls downhill, becoming bigger and bigger and causing additional masses of snow to be dislodged. The incentive to use the money monopoly for one's own enrichment is enormously seductive. And that makes it attractive to take on further debt. In the crisis, the debtors are then bailed out with the creation of more money and by the lowering of interest rates. The incentive towards a debt-based economy is further strengthened. The debt avalanche grows and grows and races faster and faster toward its ultimate destination. But the end of the road appears to be slowly coming into view. Interest rates are near zero. They cannot sink much further. State debt in most industrial nations is now at a level never seen before, during peacetime or war. Is that the economic sustainability promised on all sides?

Government deficits remain high. The unwillingness of people to radically reform the welfare state is simply too great. People are already addicted to the drug of cheap money. Banks and other financial institutions are sitting on an enormous mountain of public debt. At the same time, real and substantial economic growth is nowhere to be seen — even if that is the last shred of hope that our politicians hang on to.

The elites in politics and the banking sector are stuck in a trap of their own making. The central banks cannot allow the bankruptcy of large-scale debtors, because that could bring down the entire banking system. A government that defaults could trigger the immediate bankruptcy of the whole banking system. Raising the interest rates to a realistic level or selling the assets bought by the central banks would put at extreme risk the solvency of the banking sector, and highly-indebted enterprises, and entire governments. Not to mention over-indebted consumers …

To avoid that kind of bankruptcy, the central bank only has one option: to keep pedaling, as it were. Keeping the pedal to the metal. Producing more money to rescue debtors. But that is like throwing gasoline on a fire, because the mountain of debt and the attendant problems then continue to grow. It even appears that printing *less* money — in other words merely slowing down the money printing — (they call this "tapering") could cause substantial problems and a rash of bankruptcies for market participants.

Could there be a reduction of debt within this paper money system? In principle, yes. But a massive reduction of state expenditures for the purpose of paying down debt is pretty unlikely given the incentives for politicians in a democracy. It will instead be necessary to print more and more money so that states, banks, and over-indebted market participants do not get into trouble. Continued irresponsible behavior and a new, larger crisis are thus foreordained. This road leads ultimately to hyperinflation, which totally devalues all debt. It is *one* form of the unavoidable declaration of bankruptcy. Debtors win and creditors lose. The "paper wealth" that many built up over their entire lives will be insufficient to support the standard of living that they have imagined for themselves.

Will money just continue to be printed, and will the interest rates be stuck at zero until people totally lose their trust in paper money currencies? Will the currency collapse be inevitable, or will there be an alternative to hyperinflation? And how will the losses suffered by people play out?

Let's consider this together. Today, the central banks are feeling intense pressure to inflate the money supply.

Why? Because many economic actors that the central bank is very fond of, such as the state, whom the central bank has to thank for its position, and the banks, are over-indebted. But if that over-indebtedness can be reduced, then the pressure on the central banks to "do something" is greatly reduced.

How could the debt load of the economy be reduced? There are many ways to reduce debt. In each case, hidden losses are revealed, but in different ways. And who ultimately bears the losses may differ as well.

At one time, states could improve their financial positions just by not keeping the promises that they made. States could massively cut public pensions, social wealth transfers and unemployment insurance to pay down their deficits and to pay back their debts. Many of the state's promises of security that people relied on would turn out to be worthless.

In addition, states could simply stop paying back their debts by declaring bankruptcy. This would lead to losses at the banks and insurance companies, which have invested the savings of their customers in state bonds. When the losses already sustained come to light in this way, people will see how the value of their mutual funds and pension funds has massively fallen. State bankruptcy could — dependent on how big it is — also trigger a collapse of the banking system. A cluster of bankruptcies of over-indebted market participants would be like a financial Armageddon. For that reason, politicians do all they can to prevent that scenario.

Another path out of the debt trap is financial repression, as it is called. Financial repression means that people's savings are increasingly funneled toward the state to enable the paying off of government debt. On the one hand, financial repression makes alternative investments unattractive, for example by imposing low interest rates on savings accounts. On the other hand, it encourages the buying of state bonds. For instance, it is very attractive for life insurance companies to invest in government bonds, due to regulations that reward this behavior.

Coupled with real growth and a reduction of expenditures, financial repression could achieve a reduction of state debt. After the Second World War, the U.S. government was able to reduce its debt in relation to gross domestic product (GDP) from 130% in 1946 to 80% in 1952. But it is quite unlikely that such a trick would work now. At the time, the U.S. was at the end of a war that it had won. Government spending was sharply reduced from $118 billion in 1945 to $58 billion two years later. This occurred for the most part by reducing military expenditures. Imagine what would happen today if state expenses were halved. Everyone whose life depends on public funds would man the barricades. Over-indebted families and firms would go bankrupt in droves without the flow of money from the state. For this reason, cuts in spending similar to those in the U.S. after World War II appear to be unlikely. This is because these days, in Europe at least the majority of state expenses go not to the military, but to the welfare state. (In the U.S., they get about equal shares.)

It thus might be more effective for politicians to solve the problem of too much debt by using taxes and political measures. The idea is simple. We reduce state debt and recapitalize the banks by seizing wealth from citizens — not indirectly through inflation, but directly by taxes. The state could expropriate assets in a massive way and thus pay back state debt. What do you think about a one-time wealth tax? It might not strike fear in the hearts of investors. It is just one-time after all.

The state would sell the expropriated assets in order to pay down state debt and to recapitalize the banks. Indeed, the International Monetary Fund (IMF) recommended just that in 2013, suggesting that the EU governments put a one-time mandatory tax of 10% on all monetary assets. The goal: to bring down high government debts.

There is an even more radical method for bringing an unstable monetary system back on its feet: real monetary reform, including cancellation of state debt. This option is also very attractive and is meant to reduce over-indebtedness without provoking massive inflation. It is like pressing a "reset" button on a computer. When everything runs well, a new start in the paper money system is the result. A reform like that worked in Germany after the Second World War. (Financial repression was not an alternative in Germany after the war). The paper currency in use at the time, the Reichsmark, was replaced with the Deutschemark paper currency.

We do not want to discuss in detail the German currency reform of 1948. Just a short overview: people could exchange 60 Reichsmarks at a 1:1 ratio into D-Marks. All accounts over 60 Reichsmarks were simply divided by ten and exchanged to get D-Marks. All debts were reduced to one-tenth in value. The government's debt was declared cancelled and void, but not all debt. Can you guess who was exempted from the state's bankruptcy? That's right. State bonds held by banks were not cancelled. The banks received compensation claims. In addition to these monetary measures, a one-time wealth tax of 50% was also imposed. This careful composition of measures, taken together, brought the following positive results: Over-indebtedness was reduced, the state was practically made free of debt, the banks were recapitalized by having their liabilities reduced by 90%, but not their total assets (government bonds and real estate), and savers had their assets to a large extent expropriated. The German currency reform thus exposed to the light of day the asset destruction of the war.

An alternative to this is a "half-way" currency reform to reduce inflation, a so-called "bail-in," as was tried in Cyprus in 2013, which turned bank creditors (savers) into bank shareholders. Bank liabilities are reduced in that way and at the same time, equity was increased. The supply of money falls and bank accounts were converted into bank shares. Imagine that: One day they tell you that you cannot access your checking account anymore, but you get shares in your bank instead (that you cannot sell for a while). A bail-in recapitalizes the banking system and at the same time eliminates bad debt. Equity capital can even increase so fast that the banks might even be able to handle a partial government default. The bail-in can thus be combined to great effect with a partial elimination of state debt. In the case of a bail-in, citizens who have invested in life insurance, which in turn is invested in bank debt and government debt, are hit by the losses. As a result, the over-indebtedness of banks and government would be brought down, at the cost of savers and those holding cash money.

We do not know what the bureaucrats will choose to do in the end. In all probability it will be a mixture of some kind. But no matter what it looks like, what is not sustainable is more and more money and new debt. At some point, the end has to come. Sooner or later, the already existing losses and the illusion of wealth will be uncovered. In essence, it will be taxpayers, savers, and those holding money who will have to pay for the debt relief and to stabilize the currency.

A one-time asset tax, a currency reform or a bail-in are not popular measures, because if used, they expose the losses that exist in a brutal and immediate way. For this reason, inflation is the most popular option chosen by politicians, allowing governments to hide the cost of rescuing over-indebted economic agents.

However, the danger exists that inflation can get out of control. And we are steadily approaching that inevitable moment. The end of the road is coming into view.

The monopoly on money is like the philosopher's stone for the state. It allows the state to expand its power to an enormous extent. If inflation gets out of control and the monetary system collapses, then this power is gone. Not to mention that the real economic and thus tax losses would be massive. For this reason, it is very possible that politicians will be afraid of the inflation variant, in the end. Before we see galloping inflation, politicians will consider going with one of the other options and will try to use the "reset" button. And then we start over again from the beginning …

So are we trapped in the system? Is it possible to just keep pressing the "reset" button again and again? Is the paper money system thus not really doomed?

We have good news and bad news for you. First the bad news: So long as we have state money, bad money, we will always have too much debt. A currency reform or a bail-in could reduce the over-indebtedness for a short time, but this does not mean that the incentives for the system to self-destruct will disappear. In five, ten, or twenty years we will be in the same mess and will need the next reform. And in the meantime, tears to the social fabric, wealth redistribution, and suffering will continue.

Now the good news: in the end, the ability of the paper money system to survive into the future is dependent on how often and how much people are fooled. There is thus a way out. Abraham Lincoln once said: "You can fool all the people some of the time, and some of the people all the time, but you cannot fool all the people all the time."

But how long will it take until people understand how fiendish our current monetary system is? How much time will it take until they understand that the system allows a minority of privileged people to print money out of thin air — at the expense of the rest of us? When will people understand that the state money system is unstable in and of itself and leads to serious economic crises, to unjust redistribution, to a decline in morality, to the destruction of the family, to the expansion of the state apparatus, to poverty, and to a lack of freedom?

There is reason to hope: the more people who know the effects of state money, the harder it will be to simply push the "reset" button, because paper money in the end depends on trust. If that is lost, desperately pressing the "reset" button will not work. And then there will be the possibility of real reform — and *good money.* But only when enough people are convinced that good money is the best alternative.

We have written this book in order to get the message out. Please help us. Speak with your friends and acquaintances. Have conversations in your local clubs and meet-ups, at concerts and sporting events, at the PTA and at your local neighborhood party. The more people who know what is really happening with money, the better, for you and for us all. Getting us off this runaway train will only work if there are enough people that resist the continuation of the money monopoly game. You can do your personal part for a better world. Here and today. The effort is worth it, and a lot depends on it. May we win!

9. Why you have not heard of this before

"Whether one likes it or not, it is a fact that the main issues of present-day politics are purely economic and cannot be understood without a grasp of economic theory."

- Ludwig von Mises

Imagine that you are an entrepreneur and would like to sell an inferior product at a price that is too high. Something that older people for example would buy as a souvenir, say a cheap synthetic blanket. What would you have to do? Please think about it carefully. You would have to pull out all your shady advertising tricks. You would have to hire the best salesmen who would promote your junk product and help you lie to your customers. And you would have to be dishonest and unscrupulous. A prerequisite is that it would not bother you that you are cheating your customers. You would have to convince yourself that it is all ok. In any case, you would have to beat the advertising drum so loudly that your competition would be drowned out. And you would have to put all your effort into preventing people from getting word that your product is inferior.

And now imagine that you are the manufacturer of a high quality product that you sell in the market for a fair price, a super-soft mohair wool blanket. You would never think of cheating your customers. You have a good reputation and do not fear that anyone would make false accusations against you about your blankets.

While you can look yourself in the mirror every night with a good conscience, the unscrupulous seller on the other hand would actually have to take his mirror off the wall. Because for him, his behavior is a source of discomfort.

What do we want to tell you with this comparison? Well, it is very simple. The economic and socio-political doctrines that have gained ground in the last few decades are like *bad* products, they are *bad* doctrines. Bad ideas are being spread. For this to work, those pushing the bad ideas have to promote them constantly and aggressively with dishonest methods and propaganda. And with regularity, until everyone believes that the doctrines that have been spread are *the only correct doctrines.*

Just keep in mind that the state has no great interest in the truth about our monetary system coming out. If people knew the truth about our bad money and its effects, they would take actions to defend themselves against it. The money monopoly would collapse. And without that monopoly, things would look bleak for the state and the financial industry. Thus, the spread of bad doctrines is of enormous importance for certain groups. Primarily, in doing so, an appeal is made to people's emotions, and in Germany as elsewhere, the word "social" is certainly the adjective most over-used by politicians today.

How do you feel about the theories and ideas that we have presented to you thus far? Everything is logical, right? So logical, in fact, that no one has succeeded in proving these theories wrong.

But now the time has come to admit that we have led you a bit astray. But not in order to sell you something *bad.* In contrast, we have supplied a *good* product. *Better* ideas. For this reason, we do not suffer a bad conscience. We have also thought of the packaging and gave our book a cool title. We could have called our book *Introduction to the Monetary Theory of the Austrian School,* or *The Austrians Knew It All Along.* But would you have had any interest in a book like that, let alone bought it? Let's be honest. Not really, right? Maybe you would have thought, "my kids don't go to school in Austria, so what does the Austrian school system have to do with me? Or, what do the Austrians know that I don't know already?"

To be precise, we should have called our book *Introduction to the Monetary Theory of the Austrian School of Economics,* because that is what it is. But we didn't. Because you would have been highly unlikely to want to read the book. Who after all wants to spend their spare time reading macroeconomics? Only a few. So please be thankful that we tricked you a bit. Maybe you don't quite realize it, but with the information in this book we have put you in a position to understand and interpret the problems of our time, and most of all the effects of bad money. You will now understand this better than most mainstream economists.

We knew, by the way, that our strategy would work. The logic of the Austrian school of economics is irresistible to people who have an open mind. You have just completed a basic course in Austrian monetary and business cycle theory. Congratulations, you know more than 99.9% of the population in this field.

And why didn't you get bored reading this? (At least we assume you didn't, if you have made it this far.) Because the theory of the Austrian school is a theory of *human action.* And because we are all humans and we *all* act, we can *all* see ourselves from this point of view. The difference between the Austrian school and the mainstream schools of macroeconomic thought is — literally — the *way of thinking* about individual behavior. The Austrian school economists begin their thinking with the individual in mind, the individual person. By contrast, current macroeconomic theories mathematicise the economy. But only an equilibrium model of economics can be mathematicised — a model where the acting, creative individual has no place. Current macroeconomic theory views society and the economy as something static. It loves to deal in figures and statistics. We showed you how that worked in the calculation of the rate of consumer price increase, as an example. And the person as an *acting* individual is completely ignored there. And that is nonsense. There is never equilibrium. Billions of people have new experiences every day and learn from them. They then act differently than they would have acted that morning, an hour before, or a minute before. You will also think and act differently after reading this book. You will change your actions. You will understand and see the world through different eyes.

In his book *Memoirs*, Mises wrote:

> *"What distinguishes the Austrian school and will lend it everlasting fame is its doctrine of economic action, in contrast to one of economic equilibrium or nonaction. The Austrian school makes use of the ideas of rest and equilibrium, without which economic thought cannot get along. But it is always aware of the purely instrumental nature of these ideas. The Austrian school aims to account for prices actually paid in the market, and not just prices that might be paid under certain never-realizable conditions. It rejects the mathematical method, not because of ignorance or an aversion to mathematical accuracy, but because it does not place importance upon the detailed description of the condition of a hypothetical and static equilibrium. The Austrian school has never succumbed to the fatal illusion that values can be measured, and has never misunderstood the fact that statistical data have nothing to do with economic theory, but belong to the history of economics alone." (p. 28)*

In modern macroeconomic theory, the most simple of topics are made overly complicated, apparently with intent, so that everything appears to be very important. This intimidates people, and that is the desired result. It means that people don't ask questions, saying to themselves, "This is all too complicated for me."

But economics is in reality very simple. It functions in the same way that it did thousands of years ago. People come together to voluntarily engage in commerce with one another for their mutual benefit. People specialize and divide work among themselves to advance their condition. Would you sell something or offer a service to make your own condition worse? Of course not. This is the foundation of all action and has nothing to do with greed, which so many people want to disparage market participants for today.

This last chapter is not suitable for returning once more to our small city. But we would like to "abduct" you now for a short time and take you to another city — Vienna. Not to today's Vienna, but rather to the Vienna of ca. 1900.

Economist Carl Menger (1840–1921) is known as the founder of the *Austrian school of economics.* He wrote in his work *Principles of Economics* in 1871:

> *"Money is not an invention of the state. It is not the product of a legislative act. Even the sanction of political authority is not necessary for its existence. Certain commodities came to be money quite naturally, as the result of economic relationships that were independent of the power of the state." (pp. 261–62)*

Please read that to your banker the next time you stop by your local bank. He will laugh in your face or look at you with a puzzled expression on his face. The latter is more likely, because he will not know what you are talking about.

Carl Menger was the man who was crucial in inspiring Ludwig von Mises, the greatest economist of the 20th century. Mises, in his work *Memoirs*, writes:

> *"When I first came to the university, Carl Menger was nearing the end of his teaching career. There was little attention paid the Austrian school of economics at the university, and I had no interest in it at the time. Around Christmas, 1903, I read Menger's* Grundsätze der Volkswirtschaftslehre [Principles of Economics] *for the first time. It was through this book that I became an economist." (p. 25)*

One of Ludwig von Mises's central beliefs was that the state needed to get out of the management of money. He felt that the central bank and the state monopoly on money would have to be done away with. He would not bend or compromise on this. He was without exception or compromise a libertarian and a champion of free markets.

Mises's first career choice was the Vienna Chamber of Commerce, Trade and Industry, which he belonged to as of 1909. He was unable to attain a professorship at a public university, and that remained so for his entire life. Does that surprise anyone? They just didn't want him. Another time, he refused an offer of a well-paid position from the banking industry. Mises wrote in his *Memoirs*:

> *"After the war my expertise in money and banking was so widely recognized that many of the banks offered me a position on their boards. But until 1921 I always declined, as I was not given the assurance that my advice would be followed. Later I considered banks insolvent and irretrievably lost; events proved me right." (p. 59)*

At the same time, Mises did not want to stop teaching. His private seminar, which he held every other week from 1920 to 1934, had 20 to 25 participants, the most famous of which was Friedrich August von Hayek. Hayek would later win the Nobel Prize in Economics in 1974.

In Mises's pioneering work *The Theory of Money and Credit* — which was published more than 100 years ago — he showed that expanding the money supply has no social benefit. He did show how doing so causes a redistribution of wealth, and results in a purchasing power of money that is lower than it would have been without the increase in the money supply. And when the money expansion occurs through a credit expansion by the banking system, then a fake boom occurs, as well as malinvestment.

This is Mises's innovative and today highly relevant theory of economic boom and bust. Mises wrote about his theory of money in his *Memoirs*:

> *"As could be expected, my book was rejected by German scientific journals in a most precipitous manner. I paid little attention to this. I knew that my views would soon take hold. I saw with horror the catastrophe which I had predicted standing before the door.*
>
> *New books that are 'destroyed' by critics are lasting and valuable. He who only says what others want to hear is better off remaining silent."* (pp. 48–49)

Mises's insights were revolutionary.

In 1922, his book *Socialism: An Economic and Sociological Analysis* was published. In it, he showed that socialism cannot work, and why. And that social democracy also cannot work. This book made Mises famous immediately and also made him disliked by socialists around the world.

He said:

> *"All attempts at disproving the conclusiveness of my thesis were destined to fail." (p. 95)*

And it was exactly this inability to challenge them that brought increasing hostility from the socialist camp, as well as from the German National Socialists in the 1930s. Just an aside: National Socialism and communism are not opposites, but rather brothers in spirit. They are merely competitors of one another. Both have totalitarianism in common, and both reject the free market system.

Mises knew that the victory of National Socialism in Germany at that time would also soon threaten Austria.

After he published *Socialism,* and as a classical liberal (libertarian) and a jew, he could be certain that the Gestapo would come looking for him after a Nazi takeover of Austria. For this reason, in 1934 he left Austria to move to Geneva, Switzerland. During that time, what can be considered without a doubt his most important work was written, *Human Action: A Treatise on Economics.* In it, he developed his theory of human action, which he called praxeology. With it, contradiction-free thought and error-free thought can result in propositions that are as irrefutable as mathematical formulas.

Due to the war, the atmosphere in Switzerland in 1934 was becoming increasingly tense and thus Mises left and fled to the United States. In the meantime, the Nazis had marched into Vienna and had found Mises's entire library of books and his writings, and packed them up and transported them away. It took almost 60 years for the documents to turn up again. In the 1990s, they were discovered in an archive in Moscow. The Soviet army had confiscated them in 1945 and taken them to Moscow.

Why do we describe this in such detail? To make clear that Mises was treated badly, almost like an enemy of the state. Why was a man of knowledge and a professor treated so badly? A man who had spent his life in the service of truth? A man who stood for nothing other than *the protection of property, equality before the law, and free markets?* They thought him dangerous? Dangerous to whom? Does this list of values contain anything that *you yourself* would not support? Politicians worldwide fear what Mises said. Why? Clearly they fear being pushed aside and viewed as unimportant when people find out that state intervention in the economy and in society are at the root of our present economic problems.

You probably have asked yourself, "Why doesn't the 'Austrian' way of thinking win out by itself, if it is so clear and logical? Why have I not heard about it? There must be a catch." And the authors here are claiming that in a free market, the best "products" do tend to win out in the long run. But then, what has gone wrong?

Well, there are several reasons why a large part of the general public has not heard of the teachings of the Austrians.

The state and politicians find the teachings and theories of the Austrians *highly* disquieting. And because the Austrian school theory was never successfully shown to be false, it is simply kept hush-hush and is not taught anywhere. Not at state universities nor at other (public) schools. And some professors who claim to know with 100% certainty that theories they themselves (must) teach are the *worst* theories, are also silent about it. Anything else could very quickly represent a danger to their careers. Imagine that you were a professor at a state university and thought about questioning the state's money monopoly. Would *you* be sawing off the branch that you sit on? These subjects are taboo, they are sacred cows that cannot be touched. Even more unthinkable would be a professor defending the view of libertarian economist Hans-Herrmann Hoppe that the state is an *"expropriating property protector and a law-breaking law protector."* Do you think such a professor would have a problem with their employer? Anyone who teaches the theories of the Austrian school will have doors slammed in his face in the state-controlled education system. And he will also have problems finding a teaching position, and will have to accept reductions in income and academic reputation. Just as happened to Mises.

What is most unpleasant for the state and politicians is without a doubt the call by the Austrians for a free market monetary policy. You already know that in such a system, the political class would have access to only a small fraction of the money it now has at its disposal under our current state monopoly monetary system. In such a system, politicians would be left high and dry, like fish out of water.

The central bankers and the bankers themselves would find the banning of the creation of money out of thin air and the closing of the central banks to be very unpleasant. And who then would want to finance all the monetary theorists who publish books and essays about how state monetary policy should be formulated, and who — in many cases — have well-paid consulting jobs? It is clear why the mainstream economists defend state money. After all, they have built their intellectual careers on this error, and in most cases they have mouths to feed at home.

Economists of the Austrian school are in favor of free markets and an economy without state interference in general, not just in money. But because making laws and enacting regulations is what politicians do, it would not be long before people got the idea of getting rid of politician as a job category. A nice thought. But ... Is "politician" a real job? Someone who has made it their job to torture and rule over their fellow citizens with laws and regulations? You decide.

For the state and for politicians it is important to find someone who is responsible for all the problems in the economy and in society. Ludwig von Mises wrote this in his book *Bureaucracy*:

> *"The main propaganda trick of the supporters of the allegedly 'progressive' policy of government control is to blame capitalism for all that is unsatisfactory in present-day conditions and to extol the blessings which socialism has in store for mankind. They have never attempted to prove their fallacious dogmas or still less to refute the objections raised by economists. All they did was to call their adversaries names and to cast suspicion upon their motives. And, unfortunately, the average citizen cannot see through these stratagems." (p. 111)*

And in order for the average person to not see through the deception, the *good teachings* and the *better ideas* of the Austrians must be withheld from them. Because those proclaiming the (statist) teachings only have *bad teachings* and *bad ideas*, they have to continuously repeat them, like a broken record.

Thus, capitalism is blamed for today's problems. But does capitalism even exist anymore? The government's share of the economy in most industrial nations is close to 50%, is it not? Isn't everything regulated in almost all areas of life? We wrote about this extensively in Chapter 7. Most people associate capitalism with something negative. Anyone speaking out for capitalism today almost automatically "outs" themselves as *"un-social."* And even fewer speak out for a free market economy. "Free market economy" sounds better than "capitalism," right? But it is the same thing. Many politicians do not want to speak out against free markets. To be against free markets means — by implication — to favor state regulations. That would be bad for one's image. And because politicians fear nothing more than a bad image and don't want to be viewed as regulators, but rather as people who merely are correcting erroneous developments in the interest of the *citizens*, they need someone to blame for those erroneous developments. And that is of course not too hard, given capitalism's negative reputation. Sometimes they use the term "market failure." Can markets fail? Don't you see what kind of game is being played here?

In pursuing these goals, our benevolent defenders of the state do not shy away from using propagandistic methods. However: *Propaganda is one of the worst evils of bureaucracy and socialism.* In *Bureaucracy*, Mises cogently describes propaganda as *"always [being] the propaganda of lies, errors and superstitions."* (p. 113)

But we want to go a step further. The concept of propaganda is — in our view — still too weak to describe what politicians offer up to us every day. Demagoguery is a better term for it. Mises used that term at another point. That is exaggerated, you say? Read how author Martin Morlock defined demagoguery in his book *Die Hohe Schule der Verführung* (*The High Art of Seduction*) as follows:

> *"Anyone is using demagoguery who, at an advantageous moment promotes a political or ideological goal by flattering the masses and appealing to their feelings, instincts, and prejudices; and in addition, who is guilty of lies and promotes hatred of others, who overstates the truth, or represents things in a grossly simplified manner, portrays the thing that he is promoting as what only reasonable and good people can believe, and the way that he puts it forward or proposes to put forward as the only possible way." (p. 24)*

No other further comment should be needed here.

But why don't the representatives of the Austrian school oppose it? The question is justified.

Just try competing with those who have succeeded in gaining power over money itself. They have almost unlimited means to corrupt the people and to — above all — corrupt the opinion leaders in a society. Try competing with those who have monopolized the education system and who determine how subjects are to be taught in schools and universities. Try competing with those who write the laws and are themselves the final judges in all issues. Any questions?

In addition, let's not have any illusions. The teachings of the Austrian school are not always comfortable and easy. They insist that before money is invested, it has to first be *saved*; that before consumption there has to be production. But when, as today, there is cheap money available in the form of credit on demand, why not use it? And in this way people yield only too gladly to the temptations and promises of politicians. Democracy is also not innocent there. It gives a majority the power to steal from the minority. What else do you call it when a majority is in favor of tax increases, but those increases only affect a small part of the population, for example a tax on the rich or a wealth tax? Look at that from the point of view of a politician: If you conduct a campaign as a demagogue, you will quickly have the majority on your side.

Ludwig von Mises was always convinced that the best ideas win out in the long run. However, he did not want to change his "political way of fighting," as he called it, because he did not want to be reduced to the moral level of his opponents, in other words, to use base tactics and strategies. In *Socialism* he wrote:

> *"When nations rush blindly towards destruction, Liberalism must try to enlighten them. But even if they do not hear, whether because they are deaf or because the warning voice*

> *is too feeble, one must not seek to seduce them to the right mode of conduct by tactical and demagogic artifice. It might be possible to destroy society by demagogy. But it can never be built up by that means." (p. 418)*

The Austrian school of economics has had a kind of renaissance for some years now. Besides the original Ludwig von Mises Institute in Auburn, Alabama, there is now also a Ludwig von Mises Institute in Germany and in other countries as well, centers from which the *better* ideas are spread.

Our *main concern* is in *removing* the state's money monopoly. Yes, get rid of it. The state will not give it up voluntarily, but only under great pressure, which we can only create by working together. If this is successful, it would be a huge step forward. A great step towards smaller government, because the unlimited capacity for spending would be taken out of the hands of politicians. And with that we would have taken a decisive step towards freedom. Many of the problems that are discussed day in and day out throughout the media, spun, and commented on by the left and the right, would simply vanish into thin air. The nightly news, which are only for masochists, with their endless news stories about politics and politicians, could be reduced to five minutes. In that five minutes, everything important could be said. Imagine what you could do with the time left over!

And now to our *appeal* to you. Yes, you read that right. Our *appeal*, not our request. We call on you to help out, in spreading the teachings of the *Austrian school of economics*, and in spreading *better ideas.* What is at stake is nothing short of everyone's freedom and wealth. Concentrate first on your family and acquaintances and on enlightening them about the fact that *state* money is *bad* money. Use the social networks.

Have discussions. You now have the better arguments and they are irresistible. Anyone who you can enlighten and win over is a potential ally. And keep up on the latest editorial comments and analyses of current problems, from the Austrian point of view; for example from the Ludwig von Mises Institute in the country you live in. You will quickly find those of the same view on the Internet. There are more of them than you might think, but not enough by a long shot. The more people that view the state with distrust, the harder it will be for the state to rule over us like a nanny, to defraud us and steal from us. Join the ranks. Make Mises's motto your own — *Tu ne cede malis sed contra audentior ito* — *Do not give in to evil, but proceed ever more boldly against it.*

No one put this better than Mises himself in his book *Bureaucracy.* So we will let him have the last word here:

> *"The aim of the popularization of economic studies is not to make every man an economist. The idea is to equip the citizen for his civic functions in community life. The conflict between capitalism and totalitarianism, on the outcome of which the fate of civilization depends, will not be decided by civil wars and revolutions. It is a war of ideas. Public opinion will determine victory and defeat." (p. 115)*

Endnotes

1 In this book, the word "state" will be used to refer to government at whatever level is being discussed, usually the national level.

2 No one has researched and described the theory of human action better than Ludwig von Mises (1881–1973) in his work *Human Action: A Treatise on Economics.* Mises was the most important economist of the 20th century and the most prominent thinker in the Austrian school of economics. In this book, you will learn more about Mises and about the theory of the Austrian school.

3 In this context, the truly ruthless and malicious are those who use the monetary system itself (the monopoly on money creation) to enrich themselves at the expense of the public. This will be discussed in more detail later.

4 The unit of account function of money is important: only when businessmen can record their revenues and expenses in the same unit are they able to figure out whether their activities were profitable!

5 They would continue to use gold for other purposes of course, such as in dentistry, in electronics, and in jewelry, though without the monetary demand, the relative price of gold would fall. Only fiat paper money becomes totally worthless when no longer useful as money.

6 Actually, today most people entrust their money to a bank without even **asking** themselves whether the bank is safe. The system encourages us to act in this way with such devices as the "Member FDIC" sticker on the door.

[7] In economics, the boat and net are called "capital goods," meaning goods that are not themselves consumed, but are used to produce consumer goods.

References

Printed Literature

Baader, Roland, *Fauler Zauber [Bad Medicine]*, Resch, 1998.

Baader, Roland, *Freiheitsfunken II [Sparks of Freedom II]*, Lichtschlag, 2012.

Hoppe, Hans-Hermann, *Democracy — The God That Failed: The Economics and Politics of Monarchy, Democracy, and Natural Order.* New York: Transaction Publishers, 2001.

Hoppe, Hans-Hermann, *Der Wettbewerb der Gauner [Competition Among the Fraudsters]*, Holzinger, 2012.

Huerta de Soto, Jesús, *Money, Bank Credit and Economic Cycles*, Auburn, Ala: Ludwig von Mises Institute, 2012.

Hülsmann, Jörg Guido, *The Ethics of Money Production*, Auburn, Ala.: Ludwig von Mises Institute, 2008.

Hülsmann, Jörg Guido, *Krise der Inflationskultur [Crisis of the Culture of Inflation]*, FinanzBuch Verlag, 2013.

von Mises, Ludwig, *Human Action: A Treatise on Economics*, Auburn, Ala.: Ludwig von Mises Institute, 2000.

von Mises, Ludwig, *A Critique of Interventionism*, Auburn Ala.: Ludwig von Mises Institute, 2005.

von Mises, Ludwig, *Bureaucracy*, Auburn, Ala.: Ludwig von Mises Institute, 2005.

von Mises, Ludwig, *Socialism: An Economic and Sociological Analysis*, Auburn, Ala.: Ludwig von Mises Institute, 2006.

von Mises, Ludwig, *Memoirs*, Auburn, Ala.: Ludwig von Mises Institute, 2009.

von Mises, Ludwig, *The Theory of Money and Credit*, Auburn, Ala.: Ludwig von Mises Institute, 2009.

von Mises, Margit, *Ludwig von Mises, the Man and His Work* Philosophie, 1981.

Piketty, Thomas, *Capital in the Twenty-First Century*, Belknap Press, 2014.

Polleit, Thorsten (editor), *Ludwig von Mises. His Life and Work, for Beginners*, FinanzBuch Verlag, 2013.

Polleit, Thorsten and von Prollius, Michael, *Geldreform [Monetary Reform]*, Lichtschlag, 2010.

Rothbard, Murray Newton, *The Ethics of Liberty*, New York: New York University Press, 2003.

Rothbard, Murray Newton, *What Has Government Done to Our Money?*, Auburn, Ala.: Ludwig von Mises Institute, 2001.

Schlichter, Detlev S., *Paper Money Collapse: The Folly of Elastic Money and the Coming Monetary Breakdown*, Wiley, 2011.

Internet sources

www.bundesbank.de	German Bundesbank
www.federalreserve.gov	The Federal Reserve
www.bundesfinanzministerium.de	German Federal Ministry of Finance
www.destatis.de	German Statistical Office
www.bls.gov	U.S. Bureau of Labor Statistics
www.ecb.europa.eu/home	European Central Bank/ Eurosystem

About the authors

Philipp Bagus studied economics in Münster, Germany and in Madrid, Spain. He received his PhD under Prof. Jesús Huerta de Soto on the subject of deflation. He is a professor at the Universidad Rey Juan Carlos in Madrid. He teaches introduction to economics, principles of microeconomics and macroeconomics, and the methodology of the Austrian school. Dr. Bagus is the author of *In Defense of Deflation, The Tragedy of the Euro* and *Deep Freeze, Iceland's Economic Collapse* (Co-authored).

Andreas Marquart is chairman of the Ludwig-von-Mises-Institut Deutschland (The Ludwig von Mises Institute of Germany). After leaving school, he undertook a "classical" education at a bank and after 15 years as a banker, went freelance in 1998, now working as an investment advisor in the financial industry. His financial advice is grounded in the Austrian school of economics. You can learn more about him at: *http://austrianconsultant.de/*.

17117387R00106

Printed in Great Britain
by Amazon